INSIGHT COMPACT GUIDE

CHICAGO

Compact Guide: Chicago is a culture-based guide for a culture-based destination, revealing the splendors of the city's skyscrapers, the wealth of its museums and the excitement of its lakefront and nightlife.

This is one of more than 100 titles in Insight Guides" series of pocket-sized, easy-to-use guidebooks edited for the independent-minded traveller. Compact Guides are in essence travel encyclopedias in miniature, designed to be comprehensive yet portable, as well as up-to-date and authoritative.

GW00418149

Star Attractions

An instant reference
to some of Chicago's
most popular tourist
attractions to help
you on your way.

The Loop p17

Marshall Field p19

Picasso sculpture p22

Sears Tower p28

Board of Trade p29

The Art Institute p33

Magnificent Mile p34

Lake Michigan p39

*Museum of Science
and Industry p46*

*Frank Lloyd Wright
homes p51*

Chinatown p58

CHICAGO

Introduction

City of Broad Shoulders...**5**
Historical Highlights...**12**

Places

Tour 1: First forays in the Loop...**17**
Tour 2: Along the Chicago River to the Sears Tower **24**
Tour 3: The oldest skyscrapers in the world............................**29**
Tour 4: A stroll along the Magnificent Mile **34**
Tour 5: North along the lake...**39**
Tour 6: South along the lake...**43**
Tour 7: A round trip through Hyde Park **47**
Tour 8: On the trail of Frank Lloyd Wright..............................**51**
Tour 9: The southern suburbs...**55**

Culture

Architecture..**61**
Music and the Movies...**63**
Events Calendar **64**

Leisure

Food and Drink **67**
Nightlife **72**
Shopping **75**
Sports **77**

Practical Information

Getting There and Around **81**
Facts for the Visitor..**83**
Where to Stay...**86**

Index **88**

Chicago – City of Broad Shoulders

Opposite: a lion's welcome

Chicago is a city of strength – of bold visions, deep emotions, pungent flavors and decisive actions. Small wonder it is sometimes described as the 'city of broad shoulders', that it boasts some of the world's tallest buildings and that its traditional food dishes include various forms of protein-rich red meat.

Lincoln Park

The inhabitants of Chicago call their city the 'Queen of the Lake'. An impressive backdrop of skyscrapers majestically lines Lake Michigan and when the summer sun shines, it seems as if half of Chicago heads for the lake, creating a Copacabana of the north. Many a visitor has rubbed his eyes in disbelief at the city's magnificent location and the stunning elegance of its buildings. Culturally too, Chicago begs comparison with practically any other major world city. Its museums are wonderful examples of how art, nature, technology and history can be presented. Chicago is not just renowned for jazz and the blues, but also as the home of the world-famous Chicago Symphony Orchestra. The city has become a Mecca for modern architecture, inspiring the world's top practitioners to produce ever more astonishing structures. The world's first skyscraper was 'made in Chicago'.

Sculpture by Dubuffet

5

Chicago's rapid rise from a tiny trading post among the swamps to America's third city has been impressive. There was a time when the world of Al Capone and his gangsters was a taboo topic, but now it is accepted as an undeniable part of a turbulent history and even adds to the city's appeal to visitors. The city's past was also tarnished by industry, particularly the notorious stockyards, but readers of Upton Sinclair's *The Jungle* can be assured that the days when Chicago was the 'World's Abattoir' (Carl Sandburg) are well and truly over.

Chicago is a town that outsiders often take for granted. It is not until they begin to learn of all that it can offer that visitors start to appreciate how special Chicago is – and how much Chicagoans already appreciate it. If you look over and beyond its 'broad shoulders', you will enjoy a particularly fine urban experience.

Chicago's notorious stockyards at the turn of the century

What's in a name?

The name 'Chicago' is Native American in origin and the city is the only major American metropolis whose name remembers the one-time masters of the New World. Why those three syllables should describe the small, sluggishly-flowing river and low-lying land at its mouth is not entirely clear. The Illini or Illiniwek, a group of five Indian tribes whose name was changed to Illinois by French explorers, spoke an Algonquin dialect as did most tribes. In their language, 'getchi-ka-go' meant something big and

A Potawatomi chief

strong and 'shecaugo' meant pretty waters. To their eastern neighbors, the Potawatomies, 'choc-ca-go' was a wilderness and 'shi-kag-ong' a place where the smell of wild onions wafts through the air. In some documents from the second half of the 18th century 'Chicagou' or 'Eschikago' was described in English as 'Garlick Creek'.

Situation and size

Chicago lies at 41°50'N and 87°37'W, about the same line of latitude as Rome. On a journey from New York to San Francisco, when you reach Chicago, you will have covered about one third of a cross-country journey. The city's surface area is about 228 sq miles (591sq km), but this doubles if you include the suburbs. Situated beside the southwest shores of Lake Michigan, the fifth-largest freshwater lake in the world, Chicago is the biggest city in Illinois and the third largest in the US. Chicago city has a population of 2.78 million, but 7.3 million people live in the metropolitan area. The entire city of Chicago with 50 wards and 77 neighborhoods is located in Cook County, of which it is the administrative capital. The capital of Illinois is not Chicago, but Springfield.

Lake Michigan, one of the largest freshwater lakes in the world

Chicago was founded on the edge of the prairie on what is mainly flat, but partly marshy terrain by the Chicago River, some 577ft (176m) above sea level. The moraines which remained after the Ice Age form the main natural elevations, but altitude differences in the city do not exceed 100ft (30m). About a mile from the banks of the lake, the Chicago River forks into a southern and northern arm, splitting the city into southern, northern and western sections. However, the river has not flowed into the lake since 1900, but now passes along a canal heading towards the Mississippi River.

River of no return

The Chicago River

Some people described the huge project of diverting the course of the Chicago River as the Eighth Wonder of the World. The river was originally a tributary of Lake Michigan, and, during the 19th century, Chicagoans used it to carry sewage away into the lake, thereby polluting the source of their drinking water and spreading diseases such as typhoid. Also, a canal to the Illinois River that had existed since 1848 was too shallow for Mississippi steamers so at the end of the 19th century, there were two good reasons for the city authorities to initiate a massive engineering scheme to lower the river level and to divert its course so that it would flow into the Illinois River and then downstream to the Mississippi River. This spectacular project turned out to be a model for the Panama Canal.

Climate and when to go

Chicago is a city with distinct seasonal differences, and two principal factors determine the weather: set at the heart of a continental land mass the city endures extreme cold in the winter and high temperatures in the summer; the proximity of the lake, on the other hand, tends to moderate the extremes but contributes towards an above-average humidity level. The relatively short spring lasts from the beginning of April to the end of May and, during this period, temperatures rarely rise above 59°F (15°C) and fall at night to about freezing point. But summers are hot, usually 86°F (30°C) and above during the day. Humidity is high, although there is often a light breeze off the lake. Evenings can be cool; if you attend an evening open-air concert in Grant Park, have something warm to hand – the same applies if you go into an air-conditioned restaurant. Fall is the time of year for moderate temperatures. Until the end of October daily temperatures hover around the 50 to 68°F (10 to 20°C) region and frosts are likely from mid-October onwards. Winters are long and harsh with daily temperatures usually remaining below freezing point. At night they often dip by a further 18°F (10°C). Sudden drops in temperature can reach Arctic proportions and deep snow frequently paralyzes traffic. An icy wind whistles around the ears, unless you are wearing some kind of substantial headgear; when it turns really cold you even have to cover your face. The lake often freezes over and the blocks of ice pile up into bizarre formations. The majority of visitors choose to visit Chicago between May and September.

Chicago in the spring

Summer in the city

7

Wrap up warm in winter

City of neighborhoods

Chicago is sometimes described as the 'city of neighborhoods'. More than just a melting pot of ethnic and racial groups, Chicago's immigrants have tended to form real

Posing for the camera

A city of immigrants

communities within the various parts of the city, taking with them the social manners, values and mores of the countries from which they came.

Historically, Chicago's settlers originated from New England or Ireland. In the second half of the 19th century, most of the new arrivals were German, but these were quickly followed by Scandinavians, Poles, Czechs and Italians. In the post-slavery industrial era, the expanding mills and factories of the North brought many blacks up from the Mississippi Delta to Chicago (bringing along with them the music known as the blues, which they continued to produce in the city, but with an urban spin).

The migration varied between a trickle and a steady stream for much of the first half of the 20th century, but after World War II it became a positive flood as young blacks, often with their families, sought out the bright lights and higher-paying jobs of the city. Black people settled mainly in the south of Chicago and they now represent some 40 percent of the total population.

After World War II, the number of Hispanics from Latin America, mainly Mexico and Puerto Rico, grew rapidly until the numbers have now reached 20 percent of the total population. When new groups have arrived, they have not necessarily stayed in one place. Initially, they may have joined their fellow countrymen in certain parts of town, but as they have risen up the social ladder – after perhaps one or two generations – they have moved on, bequeathing their homes to the next wave of immigrants. Today, for example, Italians may live in an area once occupied by the Irish community.

The most recent wave of immigrants to arrive in Chicago have been Asians. Within only a short period, they have transformed whole blocks of the city into neighborhoods with the smells, sounds and sights of Bombay or Seoul. Only a few streets away there might be a completely different atmosphere, with perhaps a strong Russian influence.

During the 1940s, the city fathers began to demolish the city's ghettos and started work on communal housing projects, the most famous of which is Cabrini Green near the northern arm of the Chicago River, only a stone's throw from the Old Town neighborhood. The city authorities were proud of this urban renewal scheme, but Cabrini Green soon became a byword for poverty and crime, and the city's social problems were in time just as bad as they had been before.

Mayor Richard J. Daley also contributed to the demise of the city's unique character. He bulldozed communities, usually against their wills, in order to build expressways and plazas and universities. The business center thrived, but the city's much-loved neighborhoods were hit hard.

Economy

The economic prosperity of the city is tied up with the surrounding region and its location at the nation's crossroads. In the early days, the agricultural Midwest produced foodstuffs which were then transported across the globe via Chicago. By 1848, business was booming and local businessmen founded the Chicago Board of Trade to deal in commodities. Today, the Board of Trade, together with the Chicago Mercantile Exchange, is the center of the world's futures market.

The Board of Trade is the center of the world's futures market

Chicago's stockyards also gained worldwide fame. Here, everything from cattle 'right up to the bellow' (Upton Sinclair) was put to some industrial use. Founded in 1865, they remained in existence until 1971, when modern refrigeration systems and the development of the long-distance road network meant that a central processing system was no longer necessary. During the stockyards' heyday after World War I, the Armour company employed 25 percent of the city's workforce and slaughtered, processed, packaged and dispatched as far as Tokyo and Leningrad some 12 million carcasses per year. In 1856, sales became even easier when the Great Lakes canal system connected Chicago to the Atlantic Ocean and the city became an international port. A canal linking Chicago with the Mississippi and the Gulf of Mexico had been opened in 1848.

Harvesting wheat 20 miles from the Loop

Soon the railroads were competing with the waterways. The first track – made with English rails – was opened in 1848. Within eight years, Chicago was the biggest railroad junction in the world. Around 1865, the city started to make its own steel and the foundries continued to glow until the 1980s when worldwide recession led to the closure of most of the steel mills.

Chicago was a major railroad junction

Now, three quarters of the working population are employed in the service sector, with the state acting as the biggest employer. Major private companies include the mail-order company Sears & Roebuck, Amoco oil and Motorola, producers of electronic goods. After New York, Chicago is the main publishing center in the US. As a tourist destination, it ranks ninth with over 1 million overseas visitors. Party conventions and trade fairs attract between 2 and 4 million visitors every year.

Politics and administration

American movies have depicted Chicago's politicians as corrupt and ruthlessly ambitious. There have been many outrageous examples of personal enrichment by officials at every level from mayor down to traffic cop and back up to judge. In recent years, the press have succeeded – either by infiltration or by hidden cameras – in proving that money has changed hands for everything from the

Richard J. Daley

Richard M. Daley

*Projects like freeways kept
the business world happy*

awarding of prestigious building contracts to the inspection of restaurant kitchens. The TV documentaries which reveal the facts behind the city's political scandals are as gripping as any thriller.

Political power in Chicago is concentrated in the hands of the mayor, who is usually of Irish descent. For a mayor to hold effective power, he or she must strike a balance between the conflicting interests of the various political, economic and ethnic groups. The undisputed master at juggling these interests was the legendary Richard J. Daley, who died in 1976. He was usually known simply as 'Da Boss' or 'Hizonner Da Mare'. When Daley held this office, he was reckoned to be the most powerful person in the US after the president. He built up the local Democratic Party into an electoral machine that provided him with six victories. Every city office was occupied by one of his hand-picked supporters. He used jobs as a means of rewarding or punishing opponents and devoted his energies into making Chicago the 'city that works'.

Major projects such as urban freeways and skyscrapers kept the business world happy and communal housing was intended to guarantee the votes of the poor. When he died this finely woven network of power threatened to unravel. The first woman mayor, Jane Byrne, and the first African American, Harold Washington, followed in quick succession, but the Irish nucleus within the party machine reformed and when Washington died suddenly in 1989 only seven months after his re-election, the son of 'Hizzoner', Richard M. Daley, defeated Eugene Sawyer, Washington's successor, having skilfully exploited his father's legacy. One of 'Richie's' greatest political achievements so far – he has already been re-elected once – has been to bring the 1996 Democratic Party Convention back to Chicago for the first time since 1968.

Prohibition and Al Capone

With the beginning of Prohibition in 1920, every beer-seller, brewer and beer-drinker moved outside the law, but at the same time won a degree of social acceptance. Four years after the unpopular ban on alcohol, 15 breweries and 20,000 liquor stores were still in existence. Police raids led to a new type of bar, the 'speakeasy'. Drinkers congregated in the backrooms to drink whiskey out of tea-cups, with an agreed signal to warn of a police raid. This was the era of the bootlegger. Those who illicitly supplied alcohol joined such highly-profitable professions as gambling and prostitution, which had always survived at the margins. But these gangs were always looking to expand their markets and this led to bitter rivalries.

The long arm of the law

The most successful gangster on the Chicago scene was Al Capone (1899–1947). He wanted a monopoly over Chicago's flourishing trade in the forbidden vices. Narrowly escaping his opponents' bullets on many occasions, he was responsible for unleashing a terrifying wave of violence throughout the underworld. Between 200 and 500 gangsters died every year, and every week a bomb was detonated in one of the distilleries, bars or secret meeting-places. At times, a good half of all the city's law enforcement officers were on Capone's or other gangsters' payroll. In one year, the 'Boss' pocketed some $105 million, more than any one person had thus far earned. In his best year, Henry Ford 'only' managed to pile up around $70 million.

At the height of his power, Capone masterminded the so-called Valentine Day Massacre of 1929 which resulted in the deaths of seven members of the Moran gang. This bloodbath won him control of the Chicago underworld. But he was far from safe. At a conference in Atlantic City of all the top Mafia bosses, Al Capone was reminded that about 30 other gang leaders were challenging his monopoly in Chicago alone. In the meantime, the FBI had assembled the 'Untouchables', a group of trustworthy detectives charged with nailing the man known as 'Scarface'. 'Chicago amnesia', a remarkable phenomenon that affected the memory of all prosecution witnesses, enabled Capone to escape any murder convictions, but in 1931 he was successfully tried for tax evasion and imprisoned for a decade.

Mugshot of Al Capone

The big fish had been removed from the pond, but organized crime continued to flourish during the alcohol ban. Eventually, wise counsel prevailed and the authorities were obliged to admit the failure of the Constitutional amendment. In 1933 the prohibition on alcohol was lifted.

Al Capone died in 1947 on his estate in Florida from syphilis, partly because he could not face an injection. He was scared of the needle.

Historical Highlights

BC Lake Chicago, which covered much of what is now the American Midwest, receded with the glaciers, leaving swamps separating the vast prairies from what is now Lake Michigan.

pre-1800 Native Americans, the Potawatomi Indians, used the swampland linking the Great Lakes and the Mississippi River as a trading area. They called it 'Checagou' in reference to the stink of rotting wild onions.

1673 The French explorer, Louis Jolliet, and the missionary, Jacques Marquette, canoe together into the marshland that will become Chicago.

1779 Jean Baptiste Point du Sable, son of a black slave and a Quebec merchant, establishes a trading post on the north bank of the Chicago River, located in what is now Michigan Avenue.

1795 General 'Mad Anthony' Wayne and his troops overrun the Indians and force them to give up tribal lands, including much of what is now downtown Chicago.

1803 Fort Dearborn is built on the southern bank of the Chicago River to provide protection from the Indians and the British.

1812 Potawatomi tribes kill 52 soldiers and settlers based at Fort Dearborn. Troop reinforcements soon put down the uprising.

1816 Fort Dearborn is rebuilt.

1825 The Erie Canal opens, creating a new water route for shipping between Chicago and the East Coast.

1831 First bridge is erected over the Chicago River, linking the North and South sides of town.

1837 Chicago, now with 4,000 settlers, is incorporated as a city.

1848 The Chicago Board of Trade is established by a group of businessmen and launched as the world center for commodities trading. The first railroad (to Oak Park) and the Illinois and Michigan Canal are opened. A canal now links Lake Michigan with the Mississippi.

1855 A rebellion by German immigrants guarantees Sunday beer.

1865 Union Stock Yards, the main Chicago abattoir, is founded.

1867 George Pullman founds the Pullman Palace Car Company.

1871 The Great Fire of Chicago kills 300, leaves 100,000 homeless and destroys 18,000 buidlings in the Loop and part of the North Side. Modern Chicago emerges Phoenix-like from the ashes.

1885 The first skyscraper, designed by William Le Baron Jenney, is built.

1886 Years of discontent among the workers, including a riot outside the Pullman plant, culminate in the Haymarket Riot, when seven policemen are killed by a bomb. Four anarchists are later hanged for the bombing.

1889 Social reformer Jane Addams opens Hull House, a 'settlement house' serving the underprivileged. She is later awarded the Nobel Peace Prize.

1890 Chicago's population, heavily bolstered by European immigration, passes one million.

1892 The University of Chicago is founded.

1893 Twenty-seven million people visit the Columbian Exposition in Jackson Park.

1894 A strike by Pullman workers is broken up by federal troops.

1897 The elevated train system encompassing the Loop is completed.

1900 The flow of the Chicago River is diverted so that the city's waste will no longer run into Lake Michigan.

1905 Frank Lloyd Wright reveals plans for his architectural masterpiece, Unity Temple.

1906 Upton Sinclair's *The Jungle* describes the inhuman conditions of the stockyards.

1916 Carl Sandburg's *Chicago Poems* establishes the reputation of Chicago as the 'city of broad shoulders'.

1919 After the drowning of a black boy on a beach, racial unrest in southern Chicago leaves 40 dead. After the Chicago White Sox fail to win baseball's World Series, eight of its players, including Joe Jackson, are banned from the sport for accepting bribes to lose.

1920 Prohibition gives Al Capone the opportunity to become 'king of the underworld'. The Michigan Avenue Bridge opens.

1924 The Union Stock Yard, employing more than 30,000 workers, receives more than 18.5 million head of cattle, calves, sheep and hogs.

1929 In a garage on St Valentine's Day, seven members of rival gangs are shot dead by accomplices of Al Capone. The Wall Street stockmarket crash sends Chicago plummeting into the Great Depression.

1931 Al Capone convicted of federal income tax evasion and sentenced to eight years in prison.

1933 Chicago stages the Century of Progress World's Fair.

1934 John Dillinger, the bank robber, is gunned down by federal agents outside the Biograph Theater.

1942 As part of the Manhattan Project and under the leadership of Enrico Fermi, the first controled nuclear reaction takes place at the University of Chicago.

1947 Al Capone dies of syphilis.

1952 Hugh Hefner, circulation director of *Children's Activities* magazine, borrows $1,600 to start a new publication called *Playboy*.

1955 Richard J. Daley becomes mayor and dominates Chicago's politics for two decades.

1959 The route across the Great Lakes and through the St Lawrence Seaway becomes navigable for 650-ft (200-m) ocean-going vessels. Chicago becomes an international port.

1960 Saul Alinsky forms the Woodlawn Organization, a group that becomes the focal point for the Chicago Civil Rights Movement.

1966 The Rev. Martin Luther King Jr founds the Chicago Freedom Movement, which spawns Operation Breadbasket and Push, the groups that give the Rev. Jesse Jackson his national platform.

1968 After the death of Martin Luther King, riots hit the southern and western areas of the city. Anti-Vietnam War demonstrations at the Democratic Party Convention are brutally broken up by police and federal troops.

1971 Undercut by competition from smaller Midwestern cities, the Union Stock Yard closes.

1972 The Chicago Mercantile Exchange, established in 1919 as a tiny butter and eggs market, pioneers the financial futures markets.

1973 The 110-story Sears Tower opens and for over 20 years Chicago boasts the tallest building in the world.

1976 Mayor Daley dies in office.

1979 Jane Byrne becomes the city's first woman mayor.

1983 Harold Washington becomes the city's first Afro-American mayor.

1989 Richard M. Daley follows in his father's footsteps to become mayor. Despite decades of opposition, the Chicago Tribune Co., owners of the Cubs, install lights at Wrigley Field and the baseball team plays its first night games at home.

1991 After his re-election to office Mayor Daley vows to fight crime and ease tension as the white poulation decreases and the population of blacks and Hispanics increases.

1996 Sears Tower loses its status as the tallest building in the world to the Petronas Building in Kuala Lumpur. Democratic Party Convention returns to Chicago after 28 years.

1998 For the sixth time in the 1990s, basketball superstar Michael Jordan leads the Chicago Bulls to the NBA championship.

Lake Michigan

W. Wendell St.
W. Oak St.
E. Oak St.
E. Lake Shore Dr.
N. Rush
E.
E. Walton St.
W. Walton St.
Washington Square
E. Delaware
W. Locust St.
N. Franklin St.
N. Wells St.
N. La Salle St.
W. Chestnut St.
Michigan Ave.
DeWitt Pl.
E. Chestnut St.
N. Lake Shore Dr.
W. Chicago Ave.
N. Orleans St.
Chicago/State
Chicago
Pearson
E. Chicago Ave.
Lake Shore Park
W. Superior St.
E. Superior St.
N. Fairbanks
W. Huron St.
E. Huron St.
W. Erie St.
Clark St.
N. Dearborn St.
N. State St.
E. Erie St.
N. Wabash
N. St. Clair St.
McClurg Court
W. Ontario St.
E. Ontario St.
W. Ohio St.
E. Ohio St.
W. Grand Ave.
Grand/State
N. Rush St.
E. Grand Ave.
W. Illinois St.
E. Illinois St.
W. Hubbard St.
Chicago River
W. Kinzie St.
Merchandise Mart
E. Wacker Dr.
W. Wacker Drive
Water St.
E. South
State/Lake
Columbus
Clark/Lake
Randolph/Wabash
Illinois Center Gulf Station
W. Lake St.
N. Franklin St.
Randolph/Wells
Washington/Dearborn
Washington/State
E. Randolph Dr.
W. Randolph St.
N. Wells St.
N. La Salle St.
Clark St.
W. Washington St.
Madison/Wabash
W. Wacker Drive
W. Madison St.
LOOP
First National Plaza
E. Madison St.
Monroe/Dearborn
Monroe/State
S. Wacker Drive
S. Franklin St.
Madison/Wells
W. Monroe St.
Adams/Wabash
W. Adams St.
E. Adams St.
Grant Park
S. Wells St.
Quincy/Wells
Jackson/State
Van Buren Station
W. Jackson Blvd.
Jackson/Dearborn
Columbus
E. Jackson Dr.
S. Lake Shore Dr.
La Salle/Van Buren
W. Van Buren St.
La Salle/Congress
Eisenhower Expwy.
La Salle St. Station
Congress Pkwy.
E. Congress Drive
Harrison/State
Chicago River
W. Harrison St.
S. La Salle St.
Clark St.
S. Federal St.
S. State St.
E. Harrison St.
S. Michigan Ave.
E. Balbo Ave.
S. Sherman St.
S. Plymouth Ct.
W. Polk St.
E. 8th St.

TOURS 1–4

0   0.2 mile
0   0.2 km

N

Tour 1

First forays in the Loop

Michigan Avenue Bridge – Carbide and Carbon Building – Carson Pirie Scott Store – Palmer House – Marquette Building – James R. Thompson Center
See map on page 16

Previous pages: Chicago's skyline and canal

The Loop and the El

This walk, which will take at least a morning, leads right into the busy heart of the city, or the Loop. The Loop's name derives from the 'El' or the elevated train system that clatters around the center of the city.

Start out from the point on the Chicago River, where a fort, now demolished, was built to protect the new settlers against the Native Americans. Today, this spot is marked by a bridge which connects the Loop with the Magnificent Mile, the city's most famous shopping street.

The Loop itself is like an open-air museum documenting the history of skyscrapers. The list of architects extends from Louis H. Sullivan via Mies van der Rohe through to Helmut Jahn. A series of sculptures by world-famous artists nestle between these huge structures. As well as two large department stores, which bear witness to a century of conspicuous consumption, shoppers will find many boutiques. This central-city tour ends at a Roman-style plaza with one of the most controversial and boldest structures in the history of architecture, the James R. Thompson Center. You can conclude this tour with a trip to the top story in a glass elevator.

17

Chicago was born on the banks of a river at precisely the spot where today the **Michigan Avenue Bridge** ❶ crosses the Chicago River to link **the Loop**, the city's main business district, with the **Magnificent Mile**, one of the most exclusive shopping streets in the US. The first white people to set foot on the river's marshy banks were the French fur hunter and explorer, Louis Jolliet, and the Jesuit priest, Jacques Marquette. They crossed the river in September 1673 as they made their way to the Mississippi. In December 1681, René-Robert Cavalier Sieur de la Salle and Henri de Tonti followed at exactly the same spot. The first non-Indian settler did not arrive until exactly a hundred years later. This was the trapper and fur trader Jean Baptiste Du Sable, the son of a Quebec merchant and a black slave from Santo Domingo.

By the south bank, markers set in the sidewalk show the outline of **Fort Dearborn**. The fort, built in 1803, was initially a garrison for the US Army, but, in 1812, Indians, who wished to recapture their land, destroyed it, killed two-thirds of the people and took everyone else captive.

Jacques Marquette, one of the city's founders

Fort Dearborn

Carbide and Carbon Building

Michigan Avenue Bridge

The bridge itself was erected between 1918 and 1920. It is a fine example of the double-leaf trunnion bascule bridge so typical of the Chicago River. The bridge has two levels, one for pedestrians and one for traffic, and several times a day, ringing bells and flashing lights bring everyone to a standstill and the two halves of the bridge lift up like giant see-saws to allow tall ships to pass through. Four bas-reliefs on the bridge pylons, two by James Earle Fraser and two by Henry Hering, tell the story of the discovery, settlement, defense and finally the reconstruction of the city after the Great Fire of 1871.

To the right and facing south stands a building that was once known as the **London Guarantee Building ❷**. It dates from the 1920s and was a reaction to the purely functional appearance of many of the city's early skyscrapers, a style dismissed by supporters of the Beaux-Arts as 'commercial' or 'industrial'. The entire structure follows the pattern of a classical column: a contrasting five-story base, a tall shaft and a three-story capital are crowned with a small pavilion that is a replica of a circular Greek temple.

Also on the right and further south along Michigan Avenue, diagonally opposite the Old Republic Building, looms the ★ **Carbide and Carbon Building ❸**, an Art Deco skyscraper. Deep black in color, it looks as though it has just emerged from a coal mine. The base is in black granite, the tower clad with green but now sooty, terracotta tiles. Building regulations at the time of its construction insisted on a tapering form so that sufficient light would reach the roads and sidewalks. The polished brass rails and moldings in the lobby pick up on the external ornamentation. Look for the two intertwined letter 'C's on the elevator doors. Shiny black Belgian marble was used to frame the gray Tennessee marble on the floor and walls.

On Wabash Street the trains rattle noisily along the elevated track and around the corner. Still much loved by Chicagoans, the 'El' was inaugurated in 1892 on the occasion of the World's Columbian Exposition, which was held to celebrate the 400th anniversary of the discovery of America. The Loop was completed five years later and has changed little since then.

One six-story structure in **State Street** is dominated by a gleaming, bright-red sign. It belongs to the world-famous ★ **Chicago Theater** ❹. Above a huge lobby and pergola, the city's unofficial logo forms a stark contrast to the original building which dates from 1920. The pergola and the sign are so vast that they practically mask the unusual architectural features of the facade, whose design recalls the central arch of the Arc de Triomphe in Paris. The impact of this building was so great that the architects, Rapp & Rapp, were deluged with requests to create similar fantasy temples throughout the US. Built as a theater, it was converted into a cinema in the 1920s and is still reminiscent of the Hollywood-style neo-baroque splendor of that era. Now that the Walt Disney Corporation stages shows and musicals in the renovated theater, grown-ups and children alike can marvel at the vestibule, based on François Mansard's Sainte Chapelle in Versailles, and the fantastic 3,800-seat auditorium (tel: 312-443-1130).

Follow State Street southward and on the corner ahead you will catch sight of the green patina of one of Chicago's most famous clocks. If you say you will meet someone 'under the clock', then you mean outside the ★★ **Marshall Field and Company** store ❺, the famous department store (Friday to Wednesday 9.45am–6pm, Thursday 9.45am–7pm) and one of the few in State Street to have survived the 1980s recession. The building, which was constructed in sections by the Burnham company between 1893 and 1907, occupies a whole block and many regard it as the pinnacle of the Chicago School's architectural achievements.

Marshall Field

It is not apparent from its external simplicity, straight lines and solidity that the atriums on several levels allow lots of natural light to play on the displays inside. Climb the curving stairway to fully appreciate the magnificent **Tiffany Dome**, where 50 workers took two years to lay 1.6 million Favrile glass tiles, under the personal direction of Louis Comfort Tiffany. One very popular spot is the ice-cream parlor in the **Crystal Palace** on the seventh floor, which also offers a view over the Loop (Friday to Wednesday 10am–5pm, Thursday 10am–6pm).

Diagonally opposite stands a 'landmarked' showpiece of the Chicago School of Architecture. The ★ **Reliance Building** ❻, dating from 1891, was one of the first multi-

19

Carson Pirie Scott

Palmer House hotel

story structures to give prominence to glass. This was possible because it was supported by a skeleton of steel girders and so it was no longer necessary to give the walls a load-bearing function. The lightness which this building exudes is emphasized by broad glass bays which skilfully place the steel structure in the background and by the corner buttresses, which are faced in a way reminiscent of the pillars on Gothic cathedrals.

Another department store, the ★★ **Carson Pirie Scott and Company** store ❼, stands on the left-hand side of State Street one block further south. It was designed by Louis H. Sullivan, the most independent and also the most talented representative of the Chicago School. Sullivan's motto 'form follows function' is amply illustrated here. Unlike the Reliance Building, the wide windows are pushed into the background and the steel framework with its horizontal and vertical struts take a prominent position.

The bronze external paneling on the two lower floors is unusual – when it was built it was very controversial, as it was considered inappropriately fanciful for a downton department store. The design, which is reminiscent of Art Nouveau, was intended by Sullivan to imitate a picture frame for the store windows and the goods displayed in them. Inside, there is a forest of pillars, whose capitals pick up on the themes depicted in the external ornamentation and whose shapes are similar to Romanesque column heads (Friday to Wednesday 9.45am–6pm, Thursday 9.45am–7pm).

The ★★ **Palmer House** ❽, one block further south, is another extraordinary piece of architecture. On the corner with Monroe Street, the peacock clock and the brass embellishments in Art Nouveau recall the old C.D. Peacock's jeweler's store. The best way to approach the Palmer House is from Monroe Street and then you can walk directly on to a mezzanine floor and into the splendid lobby of a hotel now 125 years old – during those years it has been completely renovated on three occasions.

Whatever the weather, the lavishly decorated Palmer House presents the perfect opportunity to take a break. Sit down in one of the comfortable armchairs in the middle of the lobby and admire the ceiling murals by Louis Rigal and the marble clock above the entrance to the **Empire Room**. The latter is used by large companies for hospitality and is furnished in French Empire style. Mirrored walls are decorated with golden reliefs of Napoleon Bonaparte and Josephine and the impressive golden chandelier was imported from France. A shopping arcade is located on the first floor. For many, an overnight stay in the Palmer House is a nostalgic voyage into a glittering past long gone.

Turn right into West Adams Street and you will find

a gastronomic institution which has survived all the economic ups and downs of the past hundred years. Although the outside looks as if it is made of stone, it is in fact ornamental cast iron. ★ **The Berghoff** ❾ was built around the turn of the century in the style of a Bavarian beer hall. *Sauerbraten* sausages are nearly always on the menu and, if you need to quench a thirst, Berghoff's own brew of foaming beer is thoroughly recommended.

The Berghoff restaurant

21

Amply fortified, set off again towards a large square that is surrounded by huge, box-like structures made of dark glass and steel. This is the first of three plazas which provide focal points for the Loop: Federal Plaza, First National Plaza and Daley Plaza. On the **Federal Plaza**, the first thing to catch the eye is Alexander Calder's distinctive orange-red sculpture, *Flamingo*, which looks good up close and also from afar. Mies van der Rohe's **Federal Center** ❿ nearby has often been derided as an ugly duckling. The German émigré was an uncompromising devotee of the principle 'less is more'. His steel-framed structures were minimalist compositions and they represent the highlight of the 'International Style' that he embodied. He managed to create a plaza that is urbane in a thoroughly modern sense, because it succeeds without any grand gestures.

Alexander Calder's 'Flamingo'

The ★ **Marquette Building** ⓫ on the corner of Dearborn Street and Adams Street is another typical example of the Chicago School of Architecture. Its architects, William Holabird and Martin Roche, have played a part in the design of a wide variety of buildings, many of which now characterize the Chicago urban landscape. This building is shaped like the letter E, so all the rooms receive natural light. An important factor here is the use of the wide 'Chicago window'. It was devised to replace the narrower openings that were common before the use of steel girders. Above the entrance in Dearborn Street, realistic bas-reliefs by Hermon A. MacNeil depict events from expeditions undertaken by Jacques Marquette, including the one which discovered and explored the Mississippi River. Inside the two-story lobby. J.A. Holzer also produced Tiffany-style mosaics illustrating scenes from the life of this intrepid Jesuit priest. Edward Kemey's bronze reliefs above the elevator door show a number of other French explorers and Native Americans from the Mississippi valley.

Buildings on the corner of Dearborn Street and Monroe Street illustrate the development of the International Style. ★ **Xerox House** ⓬ is the work of Helmut Jahn, an enthusiastic follower of Mies van der Rohe. The rounded contours at the street corner and the towering 'penthouse' extension set Xerox House apart from all the other tall office blocks nearby. Horizontal, white-enameled bands of aluminum and silver, reflecting, double glass panels contrast with the Sullivan-style finish to the corner of the Carson Pirie Scott Building. On the north side, the glass is 75 percent transparent, on the east side only 50 percent, thus reducing energy costs. The diagonal patterns in the floor and on the hall ceiling have the effect of luring the new arrival into the lobby.

First National Bank

Beside the adjoining **First National Plaza** stands the tallest bank building in the world, the **First National Bank** with the pillars in the north and south soaring upwards but inwards, with the result that the surface area at ground level is double the space at the highest level. The square itself lies below street level and, around noon, clusters of bank employees sit on the steps and around the large fountain to eat their lunch. A large Chagall mosaic, *Les Quatre Saisons* (The Four Seasons, 1974), stands at the northeast of the plaza beneath a glass roof.

Chagall's 'Les Quatre Saisons'

★★ **Daley Plaza** ⓭, which runs north, is viewed as the heart and cultural focus of the whole of Chicago. In the summer, it is the venue for lunch-time concerts and once or twice a week farmers from the surrounding countryside come to sell their produce. If demonstrators want to draw attention to a hot political issue, then this is where they will congregate.

On the south side of the plaza, beneath what is, according to the *Guinness Book of Records*, the tallest church in the world, it is easy to overlook *Chicago* by the Catalan artist Joan Miró. This highly-stylized female form arouses as much local controversy as the untitled ★★★ *Picasso Sculpture*, consisting of 162 tons of rusted steel 50ft (15m) high. This is the biggest and heaviest of Picasso's works but, despite the scorn and derision it often receives, it has become a kind of symbol for the city. Unlike Calder's *Flamingo*, its color does not stand out against the surrounding buildings. The abstract

Miró's 'Chicago'

22

woman's head (mockingly described as a dog's head) is welded together from pieces of naturally weathering steel known as Cor-ten, matching up with the nearby **Richard J. Daley Center**, whose pillars and cross-members are covered with the same material. This building is very firmly in the Mies van der Rohe tradition. The huge span between the pillars (86ft by 47ft/26.5m by 14.5m) enables city administrative staff to change the size of the offices where they work.

In between the Daley Center and the monumental **County Building** stands a structure that has been likened to a spaceship. It houses the administrative offices of the State of Illinois and is now called the ★★★ **James R. Thompson Center** (formerly the State of Illinois Building) **14**. Although this similarly controversial edifice by Helmut Jahn is by no means the tallest building in the city, it is nevertheless of vast proportions. Its visual impact is enhanced by Jean Dubuffet's white *Monument to a Standing Beast* at the northwest corner, which is well worth a closer look. Inside the center, steps lead down from a round and airy atrium to cafés and restaurants. Glass elevators carry visitors to all levels and some of the state administrative offices overlook the inner plaza balcony-style. It is worth taking the elevator to one of the higher levels to fully appreciate the sheer scale of the plaza, which is often the venue for concerts and exhibitions.

When the center was first built, the heating and air-conditioning did not work properly. In the summer, the staff had to bring in parasols to protect themselves from the fierce sun. The Thompson Center suffered considerable negative publicity from these problems, especially as the construction costs were astronomical, but it is nevertheless and in the eyes of many a spectacular building and now one of the city's major tourist attractions.

Peering through the Picasso Sculpture

23

James R. Thompson Center and Dubuffet's 'Beast'

Michael Jordan is a man of many skills

Tour 2

Along the Chicago River to the Sears Tower

Marina City – Merchandise Mart – Rookery Building – Sears Tower *See map on page 16*

If you are not too exhausted after completing Tour 1, fitting in Tour 2 during the afternoon ought not to be a problem. The Chicago River, its bridges and waterside buildings are the dominant themes of this shorter and less strenuous walk. Apart from the newer skyscrapers on the Loop side, two buildings on the other side of the river are included in the schedule: Marina City, which seems to emerge from the river bank like two corncobs, and the Merchandise Mart, which in volume terms at its completion in 1930 was the biggest building in the world. Remember to carry your camera with you – the late-afternoon sun reflected in the glass construction on 333 Wacker Drive and the Chicago River will make a wonderful photo. The walk finishes at the Sears Tower, until 1996 the tallest building in the world. A viewing platform on the 103rd story provides an excellent vantage point: you can admire Calder's *Flamingo* from a different perspective and also watch darkness descend as a sea of lights flickers from Chicago out to the horizon and the vast prairie.

R.R. Donnelley Center

The tour begins right by the Chicago River with the ★ **R.R. Donnelley Center ⑮**, a building of 'modern Classicism' which has won many awards. Rising from a base of white Portuguese granite, this glistening, glass shaft is wrapped in vast expanses of window. At the summit of the giant 50-story column, flat roof sections somewhat reminiscent of Greek temple tympanums inset with reflecting, silver-gray glass adorn all sides. Step inside the lobby to see the interior, also designed by the architect, Ricardo Bofill. Here, reflecting water flows over black, polished basalt and three twisted columns of white marble. The marble originates from the Greek island of Thassos and is said to be the whitest natural stone in the world. At the other end of the hall, surrounded by bamboo canes, stands *Three Attorneys and a Judge* by Xavier Corberó, a sculpture sparingly carved from Catalan basalt. Another example of an artistically designed environment can be found in the super-cool **Baci** café behind the western side lobby.

On the other side of the river to the right are the two corncobs of **Marina City** ⑯. The architect Bertrand Goldberg, for a short time a pupil of Mies van der Rohe, quickly turned his back on his master's minimalist approach and sought to emphasize the social aspect of urban life. Intended for middle-income workers, this residential complex is a town within a town. As well as 900 apartments, the lower section also consists of 18 stories of garages, stores, banks, a theater, a rollerskating rink, a swimming pool, fitness rooms, a TV studio and a landing stage for motor boats and yachts. Like slices of cake, the apartments become narrower towards the center, where the elevators are situated. There is a spectacular view of the Loop from the rounded riverside balconies.

Marina City

Follow the promenade westwards along the north bank of the river as far as LaSalle Street. Here it is well worth taking a detour to the north to discover one of Chicago's newest and most fashionable spots: ★ **Michael Jordan's Restaurant** ⑰ on the corner with Illinois Street. Dedicated to the best basketball player and sportsman in the US, perhaps in the world, possibly even of all time, it attracts young people and those who have stayed young, who come to watch the big games live on giant screens behind the bar. A store next door sells sports merchandise and on the upper floor a restaurant serves Michael Jordan's favorite dishes, like steak, chicken, pasta and absolutely enormous salads.

Following Wells Street back towards the river, the tour passes a building which, in terms of office space, is only surpassed by the gigantic Pentagon in Washington; it even has its own zip code. The two lower floors of the ★★ **Merchandise Mart** ⑱ is given over to retail outlets, cafés, snack bars and restaurants. Major furnishings, furniture and interior design companies occupy the 1,200 or more offices and showrooms on the top floors. In order to keep the building with its 4,000 windows cool during the summer, over 900 tons of water is turned into ice every night using off-peak cheap-rate electricity. In the lobby at the top floor level, 19 fabulous pastel-shaded frescoes by Jules

Merchandise Mart

333 West Wacker Drive

Civic Opera House

Guerin show the industries, products and landscapes of the world's main trading nations. If you wish to visit the upper floors, then arrive here around noon and you can join a guided tour. This Art Deco colossus, which was commissioned by Marshall Field in 1930, became the property of the Kennedy family after World War II. In 1953 John F. Kennedy, later to become the President of the United States, unveiled the gallery of gleaming gold busts portraying Chicago's captains of industry, on the river side of the complex. The brightly-lit Merchandise Mart is at its most spectacular at night.

From the Merchandise Mart concourse, you can see a segment-shaped glass construction on the other side of the river. ★ **333 West Wacker Drive ⓳**, another award-winning structure, follows the bend in the Chicago River and fits in with the checkerboard pattern of the streets. A mantle of glass hides the interlaced girders of the steel skeleton. Walk around the circular flower-bed and observe the constantly changing reflections.

Follow busy Wacker Drive south. The grand **Civic Opera House ⓴** between Washington Street and Madison Street is a combination of genuine Art Deco and imitation French Renaissance. Its lobby, which occupies the length of the building, can be reached from the arcades along the east side. Primarily an office block, in the northern wing there is a theater with seating for 900 people and, at the other end, an opera auditorium with 3,500 seats. The much-loved **Chicago Lyric Opera** is based here. Each season (September to February) the theater management adheres to a long-established tradition of presenting works by two modern American composers as well as the usual classical repertoire. The building itself was commissioned in 1929 by Samuel Insull, one of the city's most unscrupulous but wealthiest entrepreneurs. He made his money out of energy companies and railroad lines and then lost it all during the Depression.

★ **One South Wacker Drive ㉑**, an office block situated diagonally opposite, was completed in 1982 and is another of Helmut Jahn's works. He had to limit the number of stories to 40 because the earth beneath was not capable of supporting a heavier load. The most striking feature is an asymmetrical kink in the facade, which in two places is set back by one structural section. In each case, the oblique extends over three levels, allowing the creation of bright atriums. From the outside, these spaces can be identified by copper-colored glass panels. At the edges and around the upward-pointing windows the outer walls are finished in black glass with a metallic coating.

Turning into Madison Street just before Jahn's building, two blocks along on the left-hand side and slightly set back from the road is the ★ **Madison Plaza complex ㉒**.

It was created by one of Chicago's busiest architectural companies, Skidmore, Owings & Merrill, or SOM. It took only a short time to complete as large prefabricated load-bearing sections were used in order to minimize the amount of welding work that needed to be done on site. The building, whose notched saw blade silhouette draws the eye upward, allows space for a small square, where Louise Nevelson's black steel sculpture *Dawn Shadows* is situated. It is intended to replicate the brief impression that an El train makes on the reflective outer wall of the skyscraper as it comes around the corner.

One block further east, turn south into LaSalle Street, the street of high finance. At the end of this canyon, the bright aluminum but faceless goddess of agriculture, Ceres, dominates the roofline of the Chicago Board of Trade Building (*see Tour 3, page 29*).

One building on LaSalle Street particularly worth closer inspection is the reddish-brown ★★ **Rookery Building** ㉓. It was completed in 1888 under the direction of Messrs. Burnham & Root and its lobby was altered by Frank Lloyd Wright in 1907. The last, comprehensive renovation project was finished in 1992. This edifice belongs to the first generation of skyscrapers, as its external walls have a load-bearing function, while cast-iron pillars and wrought-iron girders were employed inside. It is finished in reddish brown terracotta. Note the street names on the corners with their Art Nouveau ornamentation. Small turrets, coarse rustication and rounded arches above the windows lend the neo-Romanesque air that the much-admired architect Henry Hobson Richardson had intended. This contrasts sharply with the lobby, where banisters, staircases and the beams for the glass ceiling above the stairwell wonderfully illustrate the turn-of-the-century style

The Rookery

The sky's the limit here

28

The soaring Sears Tower

*From the Skydeck
you can see four states*

with its elegant glass and cast-iron construction methods. Wright's influential hand is clearly evident in the design of the lamps. The ornamentation can be admired in peace at the **Wall Street Deli**, which closes at 5pm.

Now is a good time to make the breathtaking ascent of the ★★★ **Sears Tower** ㉔, but before making straight for the entrance to the elevator on Jackson Boulevard, go to the west side of the building to admire Alexander Calder's colorful sculpture *Universe* on the lobby wall.

When you pay to ride up to the **Skydeck** (winter 9am–10pm, summer 9am–11pm), included in the price is a visit to the basement exhibition about the 10 finest buildings in the city and also an introductory video. On the Skydeck itself, tape loops point out some of the sights.

The Sears Tower took three years to build, and from 1973 to 1996, at 1,453ft (443m) it was the tallest building in the world, a title now claimed by the Petronas Building in Kuala Lumpur (1,610ft/491m). Its great height was possible thanks to very strong anchorage. Nine steel-framed cubes reaching up to the 50th floor stand on a concrete base, itself resting on 114 firmly anchored caissons. Above the first nine cubes are seven, then five and finally, for the top section, only two cubes, each one providing stability against the wind. The building has 110 floors, the structural steel weighs 76,000 tons and the whole edifice 225,000 tons. Eight times a year automatic machines wipe the 16,000 tinted windows clean for the 25,000 staff.

Of all the superlatives that apply to Sears Tower, the finest of all occurs on a clear evening, when the sun sinks down low in the sky and sends its last shafts of light up on to the reflecting surfaces of the skyscraper. If you have waited a long time for that, then you should wait just a little longer, until the glimmering network of expressways disappears on the dark and distant horizon.

Tour 3

The oldest skyscrapers in the world

Chicago Board of Trade Building – Monadnock Building – Harold Washington Library Center – Auditorium Building – Art Institute of Chicago
See map on page 16

The main focal points for this tour provide some fine examples of early skyscraper architecture. It will become clear what precisely were the problems of reaching for the sky and how the first pioneers of the Chicago School solved those problems. At the start, you can step inside the city's stock exchange, the Chicago Board of Trade. If you are more interested in the turbulent events on the trading floor than Art Deco buildings, make sure you are there in the morning. The first building of historic interest is the Monadnock Building, a building that predates the first generation of skyscrapers. If you think you are spending too much time staring up into the sky, you can try a detour by bus or by cab up to the **Prairie Avenue Historic District** (duration: 3 to 3½ hours), a luxurious residential area where Chicago's high society lived at the turn of the century (visits Wednesday to Sunday only). You can terminate this half-day walk (without detour) either in Grant Park, with a lecture or a concert in the Art Institute or in one of the many cafés in Michigan Avenue.

Designed by Holabird & Root and completed in 1930, the soaring ★★★ **Chicago Board of Trade Building** ㉕ is not only one of the finest Art Deco skyscrapers in the world, but also houses the world's oldest and busiest futures exchange. Broken up vertically and stepped horizontally in typical Art Deco fashion, the structure is crowned by the almost 33-ft (10-m) high Ceres, the goddess of agriculture. Its limestone base is adorned with reliefs consisting of a clock surrounded by an allegorical figure representing time and a Native American (the former bearing ears of wheat, the latter corncobs) by the sculptor Alvin Meyer of Illinois.

Chicago Board of Trade Building

The lobby is paneled with black and yellow-brown marble and a waterfall motif is repeated in various forms. The annex, designed by Helmut Jahn and completed in 1980, adopts Art Deco themes but uses modern materials. The tall atrium on the 12th floor of the annex contains a figurative impression of Ceres painted by local artist John Warner Norton. This painting originally adorned one of the trading rooms in the old section.

Spectators can observe the frantic proceedings on the trading floor from a gallery and a brochure unravels the

Frenzy on the trading floor

mysteries of the traders' gestures (Monday to Friday 9am–1.15pm).

If you missed out on breakfast or are ready for a rest and lunch, then try **Cellers Market**. It is located in the basement and feeds up to 3,500 people with home-made fare. The **Ceres Café** just off the lobby is popular with the stock exchange traders who often stop off here for a drink before heading home.

Monadnock Building

Follow Jackson Boulevard eastward. Before Dearborn Street stands the gloomy ★ **Monadnock Building** ㉖ designed by Burnham & Root (1891) – the southern wing by Holabird & Roche was added in 1893. Its north section, 200ft (60m) high and 200ft (60m) long is the tallest Chicago building with load-bearing walls. Simple bay windows provide the only ornamentation on the brick facade. The southern wing maintains the external uniformity of the building – a steel skeleton is concealed within.

If you follow Dearborn Street to the south, you will come to the **Fisher Building** ㉗ by D.H. Burnham & Co. This steel frame construction bears some resemblance to the Reliance Building (*see Tour 1, page 19*), although the ornamentation is neo-Gothic in character with yellow terracotta fish, salamanders, mussels and shrimps as the dominant theme. But the decorations are so discreet that the character of the structure is not lost. If you look closely you will see that the southern wing of the building is stabilized by the northern section. Anchoring foundations in soft loam always proved to be a problem in the early days of skyscraper construction.

Old Colony Building

The ★ **Old Colony Building** ㉘ by Holabird & Roche (1894) lies to the south of Van Buren Street. Note the rounded oriel windows at the corners – invariably, this bright room was earmarked for the boss. Holabird & Roche not only devised the Chicago window, which let in plenty of daylight, but in the Old Colony Building they employed strengthening techniques that had been previously used in bridge construction to protect against wind pressure. It is interesting to observe how the architects have sought to emphasize the vertical lines on one side of the building, the horizontal lines on the other.

A few steps away from the Old Colony Building, separated only by the narrow, neo-Gothic Plymouth Building, stands the **Manhattan Building** ㉙ by William Le Baron Jenney (1890). For a short time this ranked as the tallest building in the world and it was also one of the first of this height to use skeleton construction methods throughout. Even the walls of the neighboring property are incorporated into the shell. The purpose of the ledge at the 10th floor is to reduce the pressure on the adjacent building. Jenney often used metal girders – he was sometimes regarded more as an engineer than an architect. He is credited with the honor of having built the Home Insurance Building, the first skyscraper in the world which has since been demolished.

If you look over to the west, you will see an unusual, triangular building, whose facade resembles one of those punched cards that date from the early days of computers. It is the **Metropolitan Correctional Center**, where convicted prisoners or those awaiting trail are held temporarily. Harry Weese, the architect, designed each cell with a 5-inch (12cm) wide opening – this is the maximum permitted width for windows with bars. The windows in the administrative block below are more than twice as wide. On the top floors, 44 cells are grouped around each landing and this is supervised by one unarmed guard. The volleyball and basketball courts, for use during the prisoners' recreation periods, are not completely out in the open, as they are fitted with a specially designed wire cover to prevent helicopter-assisted escape bids.

Correct behavior keeps you out of here

On the other side of the Expressway stands the more cheerful ★★ **Printer's Row** ⓿ comprising various historic buildings and some fine restaurants. As the name suggests, printing works and publishing house once occupied this site. At that time, factory designs were influenced by the neo-Romanesque ideas of Henry Hobson Richardson and this style can easily be identified on the **Donohue Building** at the southern end of Printer's Row. It has columns and coarse rustication on the doorway. Prairie House Style influences are also evident on the finest of the buildings here, the **Franklin Building** opposite. Architect George C. Nimmons had glazed tiles set into the brick facade to form geometric patterns. A mural above the entrance shows the first print of a document in a medieval setting. There is a café inside where you can take breakfast or enjoy a healthy lunch.

Printer's Row **31**

Printer's Row is now a residential street, but it boasts a number of watering holes, including two Italian, one Thai and one Irish pub. In addition, there is **Blackie's**, a bar with a history. Celebrities such as Glenn Miller, Rocky Marciano and the Marx Brothers were regular customers here. Other bars and a youth hostel are situated close to **Dearborn Station**, recently converted into a shopping center.

By Congress Parkway, the post-modern building with strange-looking, green metal owls crouching on its roof is the ★★ **Harold Washington Library Center** ⓿. Completed in 1991, it is the biggest library building in the US and one of the world's great public libraries (Sunday 1–5pm, Monday 9am–7pm, Tuesday and Thursday 11am–7pm, Wednesday, Friday and Saturday 9am–5pm; guided

The largest library building in the US

Inside the Auditorium

tours Monday to Saturday noon and 2pm, Sunday 2pm). Each of the six grandly equipped stories is tastefully decorated with modern art exhibits. When you enter the delightful, brightly-lit winter garden on the 9th floor, then the impression of vastness that is evident from outside soon disappears. Enjoy lunch in the airy **Beyond Words** restaurant on the same floor or return to a lower floor for refreshments in the **Uncommon Ground** café and a look around the old library book stall and gift store.

The **Leiter Building II** 32 by William Le Baron Jenney (1891), which adjoins to the east, is now known as **One Congress Center**. It was commissioned by a business partner of Marshall Field, Levi Z. Leiter. Jenney abandoned all classical pretensions and concentrated on a utilitarian building with straight lines. The columns rise without interruption up to the roof cornice and the facing clearly reveals the steel skeleton. Large windows allow plenty of daylight to enter. Its simple functional qualities are reminiscent of a warehouse or a factory.

Further east along Congress Parkway by Grant Park, Adler and Sullivan's ★★ **Auditorium Building** 33 reflects the influences of Henry Hobson Richardson. Now both a hotel and a theater for 4,300 people (tel: 312-902-1500), until the 1930s it was the home of the Chicago Opera. The popularity of the opulently decorated auditorium is down to excellent views of the stage and fine acoustics. Louis H. Sullivan's overall scheme and Adler's internal decorations were much discussed in architectural circles and helped establish Sullivan's reputation as the 'Father of Modernism'.

One of the last stops along this walk is at the **Fine Arts Building** 34 by S.S. Beman. Solon Spencer Beman, famous for building the Pullman workers' district on Chicago's southern periphery, designed and constructed

Fine Arts Building

the block originally as office accommodation. It now houses four theaters, high-ceiling studios, rooms for rehearsals, stores and offices. This, the Auditorium Building and the **Orchestra Hall**, two blocks further north, form the city's creative heartland. It was here that the first editions of the literary magazines *Dial* and *Poetry* were published. The Little Theater introduced Chicagoans to George Bernard Shaw and L. Frank Baum, the author of *The Wizard of Oz*, had an office here. For a time, architect Frank Lloyd Wright and sculptor Loredo Taft used studios on the 10th floor. These rooms are 22ft (7m) high and fitted with strong overhead lights. Despite all the traffic, it is sometimes possible to hear the sound of young talent coming from somewhere in the building.

Relaxing in Grant Park

Now you can relax in **Grant Park**, rest in one of the sidewalk cafés on Michigan Avenue or else pay a visit to one of the world's top art galleries, the ★★★ **Art Institute of Chicago** ⑮ (Monday to Friday 10.30am–4.30pm Tuesday 10.30am–7.30pm, Saturday 10am–5pm, Sunday noon–5pm; guided tours daily at 2pm). It may be you want to listen to a lecture (usually Friday) or perhaps sip coffee in the atrium to the accompaniment of traditional jazz (Tuesday afternoon). If you just want something to eat or drink, use the Grant Park entrance. To fully appreciate the art treasures, you should set aside at least a day.

Beaux Arts detail, Art Institute

33

The building itself was designed for the 1893 Columbian Exposition and intended for use as a museum afterwards. Shepley, Rutan & Coolidge, the architects, implemented a plan in the Beaux Arts style drawn up earlier by John Root. The lions with the green patina that flank the entrance are the work of Edward Kemey and now serve as a symbol for the museum.

The museum contains Old and New World art treasures spanning 5,000 years of history. Probably the highlight for most visitors is the collection of European art since the Renaissance, including the third largest collection (after Rome and Paris) of French Impressionist and post-Impressionist paintings. However, the excellent collection of Asiatic objets d'art and sacred artifacts from early times right up to the present day are also highly prized. The collection of American art comprises cult paintings such as Grant Wood's *American Gothic* and Edward Hopper's *Nighthawks*. Fine examples of European craftsmanship include Meissen porcelain, Bohemian glass and Bauhaus furniture. Photography, prints, drawings, textiles and architecture also feature prominently. Other smaller collections are centered around ancient objets d'art, medieval weapons and pre-Columbian American art. Special exhibitions, some of them unique experiences in the art world, draw visitors from every continent.

Magnificent jewels

Tour 4

A stroll along the Magnificent Mile

Chicago Cultural Center – Wrigley Building – Chicago Tribune Tower – John Hancock Center
See map on page 16

For many, glitzy Michigan Avenue, often referred to as the Magnificent Mile, is the finest shopping street in the US. If you want to know what Chicago and the rest of the world regard as the current trends in (usually European) haute couture, then amble down the sunny side of this grand avenue and let your eyes wander. Do not let the fact that from the outside many of the buildings, such as Water Tower Place, look rather plain and unexciting. Inside they gleam and glitter. At the point where Michigan Avenue narrows slightly, look for the neo-Gothic Water Tower, an unshakeable symbol of Chicago's endurance; it was the only structure in the district that survived the Great Fire of 1871.

Serenading the shoppers

Conclude this shopping trip – allow at least half a day, shopaholics even more – with a climb to the top of Chicago's third highest building, the John Hancock Center. Then, with cocktail in hand, you can survey this magnificent boulevard (and much more) from on high.

From the Art Institute of Chicago (*see Tour 3, page 33*) a line of tall office blocks runs along the left side of Michigan Avenue, ending, for the moment, with the ★ **Chicago Cultural Center** ❸❻, a neoclassical edifice dating from 1897 and stylistically resembling the Art Institute. Until the completion of the Harold Washington Library Center, this building served as the city's public library, but it is now a venue for a wide range of cultural events, including exhibitions, lectures and concerts of every kind. A tour of the building with expert guides takes place every Tuesday and Wednesday at 1.30pm and every Saturday at 2pm. A monthly program, together with other information and a map of the Loop, is available from the Visitor Information Center (Monday to Friday 10am–6pm, Saturday 10am–5pm, Sunday noon–5pm, tel: 312-346-3278).

The ★ **Stone Container Building** ㊲, again on the left side of Michigan Avenue, is another unusual skyscraper. Its most striking feature is the oblique 45° cut across the top, so that when viewed from Grant Park what you see is a huge diamond. Some architects have criticized it, claiming it is out of place. A slim sculpture at ground level changes color and pattern as you walk round it. This is ***Communication** X-9* by Yaacov Agam (1983). Diagonally opposite, one block further north, the ***Splash***, a colorful aluminum sculpture by Jerry Peart (1986), occupies a small plaza.

Stone Container Building, on the left

The stretch from here to the bridge was covered in Tour 1. The **Magnificent Mile**, otherwise known as the 'Boul Mich', starts on the other side of the bridge. Just to the left stands the cream-colored ★★ **Wrigley Building** ㊳. Completed in 1919, it occupies one of the most prominent sites in the city and accordingly ranks as one of Chicago's most ornate edifices. William Wrigley, the soap to chewing gum king, wanted his company headquarters to become a landmark and the design was modeled on the White City of the 1893 Columbian Exposition. The tower is a replica of the Giralda Tower in Seville. An annex dating from 1924 fits in so well that it underlines the impression of the main structure. A peaceful patio with a fountain connects the two buildings.

Wrigley Building and Tribune Tower

Opposite stands the ★ **Chicago Tribune Tower** ㊴, the home of the *Chicago Tribune*, once the largest-circulation daily journal in the US. This vast building was completed in 1925 after a nationwide competition in which Walter Gropius and the Finnish architect Eliel Saarinen (2nd place), took part. The newspaper's foreign correspondents were given the job of acquiring fragments of all the important buildings in the world and this comprehensive collection can be seen embedded in the outside wall with accompanying information for each one. In the annex to the north at **Hammacher & Schlemmer** you can look at and buy the sort of things you did not know you needed, such as automatic swimming pool cleaners.

Tribune tribute

Below Michigan Avenue, there is another level of traffic. Down there, in what has become one of Chicago's legendary bars, journalists and editorial staff from the nearby publishing companies meet during their spare time. The

Billy Goat Tavern

original proprietor of the **Billy Goat Tavern**, now dead, was one of Chicago's originals. William 'Billygoat' Sianis owned a goat and, although his four-legged friend was in possession of a ticket, it was banned from entering Wrigley Stadium. Outraged, the goat and bar owner put a curse on the Chicago Cubs and their long-suffering supporters are still waiting for the spell to be exorcised.

The grand **Hotel Inter-Continental** ❹, in the former club-house of the Medinah Athletic Club, is crowned by a golden dome. While a neo-Egyptian design predominates outside, the lobbies, bars, lounges and halls on all floors exhibit the faded charm of past eras and distant cultures. If you can afford to stay here, then do not miss the indoor pool on the 14th floor. The luxurious fin-de-siècle pool can become almost addictive.

On the right-hand side beyond Grand Avenue, **Timberland** seeks to lure customers into its elegant premises. In line with his Beaux-Arts training, Philip B. Maher provided the facade with exquisite female reliefs. The whole building was originally commissioned by a women's outfitter. Opposite on the west side is the **Marriott Hotel**.

36

The next block on the left is occupied by a complex comprising a restaurant and several fashion boutiques, including a Levi's, and a multiplex cinema with nine screens. Several buildings which enjoyed 'landmark' status, including one with a Mies van der Rohe interior, were sacrificed to the project, despite a fierce campaign by preservation societies. On the east side stands **Bigsby & Kruthers** menswear store.

The sidewalks beyond Ontario Street are flanked by a number of high-class stores. On the right-hand side is **Burberrys**, purveyors of traditional elegance, while to the left **Cartier** in another Beaux-Arts building by Maher appeals to the affluent with Parisian chic. The bright premises of **Crate & Barrel** next door are among the most modern in Michigan Avenue. This kitchenware company sells everything from pots and pans to complete interior design packages.

Terra Museum exhibit

Niketown sculpture

Philip B. Maher, whose works are amply represented in Michigan Avenue, is also responsible for a slender building just beyond Erie Street, where the ★ **Terra Museum of American Art** ❹ is housed (Tuesday noon–8pm, Wednesday to Saturday 10am–5pm, Sunday noon–5pm. Guided tours: Tuesday to Saturday at noon and 2pm). The museum specializes in exhibiting the works of less-well-known American artists from the last two centuries; occasionally, the gallery holds special exhibitions of works by inner-city and suburban artists. Young people probably prefer to head for **Niketown** opposite, where gray sculptures of sportsmen jump out from the outside wall.

Shop here for shirts

On the northwest corner of Huron Street and Michigan Avenue, **Chicago Place** ㊷, with **Saks Fifth Avenue** at its heart, welcomes the fashion-conscious. **Allerton**, a huge brick-built hotel on the opposite side, opened in 1924 to accommodate men and women traveling alone. As well as **Brooks Brothers**, whose suits F. Scott Fitzgerald (according to Hemingway) was wearing in Paris during the 1920s, there is **Tiffany & Co** exhibiting typical understatement in its small, but exquisite window displays. Enter if you're feeling wealthy and elegant. On the other side of Superior Street, **Neiman Marcus** occupies a four-story cube. Enter via a large round doorway.

The Water Tower

The 154-ft (47-m) high, neo-Gothic ★ **Water Tower** ㊸ may look totally out of place, but it has become a symbol for the city. It was built in 1869 and was described as fireproof. When the Great Fire laid waste the rest of the city two years later, the Water Tower did indeed survive, in fact it was one of very few that did, although the waterworks engineer first had to cut the sails from several of the boats on Lake Michigan, soak them in water and wrap them around the tower.

37

Oscar Wilde, who was fascinated by the modern machinery in the pumping station opposite, mocked the tower's architecture. He called it a 'castellated monstrosity with pepper boxes stuck all over it'. In the 1930s the city fathers wanted to demolish the building to allow the road to be straightened, but the voice of protest won through: the Water Tower is now a protected monument and serves as a busy **tourist information center** (open Monday to Friday 9.30am–7pm, Saturday 10am–7pm, Sunday 11am–5pm).

To escape the shopping frenzy for a while, consider heading east along Chicago Avenue or Chestnut Street to another gem in Chicago's museum selection: the new ★ **Museum of Contemporary Art (MCA)** ㊹ (Tuesday, Thursday to Sunday 10am–6pm, Wednesday 11 am–9pm; closed Monday). Since 1996, this design by German architect, Josef Paul Kleihue, has been the home for works by Max Ernst, René Magritte, Joan Miró, Andy Warhol, Josef Beuys and a number of younger artists.

Water Tower Place has 150 stores

In ★ **Water Tower Place** ㊺, the urge to spend can be satisfied in gleaming splendor. Externally the building may look extremely restrained, but inside shoppers will be diverted by the gleaming luxury above the staircases, atriums and elevators. The center comprises over 150 fashion boutiques and other retail outlets, cafés, restaurants, cinemas and agencies and Marshall Field & Co have another department store here, too. If you want to get away from the hustle and bustle, then pay a visit to the lounge in the **Ritz-Carlton**. Up on the 12th floor (access via Pear-

John Hancock Center

'Playboy' started in Chicago

son Street), you can sample culinary delights beside a splashing fountain in a huge, tropical-style conservatory.

However, you may find that the café in the **Borders** bookstore on the other side of Water Tower Place puts less strain on the purse. Few children willingly let their parents pass the **FAO Schwarz** toystore next door, which seems to sell every toy in the world.

The ★★ **John Hancock Center ⁴⁶** is the third-largest building in Chicago and, if you make the ascent to the top floor, you will find the view equally as stunning as that from the Sears Tower (*see Tour 2, page 28*). There is an observation deck on the 94th floor, but many people prefer to look down on the miniaturized city below from the restaurant on the 95/96th floor – although the prices do match the altitude! If, after a hectic day's shopping, a cocktail would hit the spot, then this is the place to go.

Holabird & Root's **Playboy Building ⁴⁷** on the right, a typical example of Art Deco, is the headquarters of the men's magazine, *Playboy*, established in Chicago by Hugh Hefner in 1953. On the other side of Michigan Avenue stands the luxury **Four Seasons Hotel** – the same building contains a branch of Bloomingdales, the famous New York department store, but loyal Chicagoans do seem reluctant to cross its threshold. **Gucci**, on the corner, faces **Chanel** on the other side of Walton Street. **One Magnificent Mile** marks the end of the shopping street. This is where you will find **Spiaggia**, probably Chicago's top Italian restaurant. As well as the northern Italian home-made pastas and brick-oven pizzas, diners love the view over the lake and Oak Street Beach. You can enjoy the same view from the café next door but will not need to reserve a table. The desserts and cakes here are irresistible.

The **Drake Hotel** on the east side of the street is a Chicago institution that dates from the 1920s. You may not be able to afford to stay here, but you can at least enjoy an evening of jazz in the grandly furnished lobby.

After a day of shopping, only the fittest will be in the mood for one of the wild and raucous **Rush Street** bars. But in fact you will not find only smoke-filled taverns here – there are a number of relaxing sidewalk cafés too. To explore the Rush Street scene, turn to the west off Michigan Avenue along Oak Street. (Incidentally, one section of Oak Street boasts a range of small high-fashion stores, such as **Armani**, **Sanders** and **Versace**.) The Rush Street bars are found between Chicago Avenue and Division Street and in the first block of Division Street to the west. The new heart of Chicago's nightlife, with bars and restaurants such as **Excalibur**, the **Hard Rock Cafe**, **Rock'n'Roll MacDonalds**, **Planet Hollywood** and **Ed's** – is located in the Ontario Street area to the west of Michigan Avenue.

Tour 5

North along the lake

Oak Street Beach – Lake Shore Drive – Chicago Historical Society – Lincoln Park *See map on page 40*

Chicago's central beach, Oak Street Beach, is at the point where the north end of Michigan Avenue meets busy but beautiful Lake Shore Drive. From here, either on a bike or on rollerblades, you can follow the shores of Lake Michigan along purpose-built paths in both directions, but you will be sharing the experience with joggers and walkers and at the weekend the northern section in particular can become very crowded. Even at the chess pavilion, it is not always easy for players to concentrate on the game, when there is so much activity. At the southern end of Lincoln Park, one building is devoted to the history of Chicago. The zoo and small farm are very popular with both young and old, but after that, cyclists and skaters will probably find the going a bit easier. The lakeside path passes marinas and various sports arenas.

If you stop off from time to time or take a break for a picnic, this walk will easily last an afternoon but if, at the end, you want to make a short detour into the fashionable area around Belmont Avenue, it is worth setting aside a day. Then you will be able to take your time watching the world go by from one of the trendy sidewalk cafés. In the evening, you could watch a play in one of the theaters, or go to a blues club or a bar with live music.

A bike is not essential. You can walk, but allow an extra three hours. The return journey from Belmont is easy either by bus or on the El. Expect to cycle about 12 miles (20km); the stroll through the Lakeview district covers about 2½ miles (4km).

Cooler by the lake

Beach babes

★★★ Oak Street Beach 48 is bordered on two sides by skyscrapers and skirted by traffic trundling along **Lake Shore Drive**. Lake Shore Drive is one of the city's 'showcase streets'; its huge homes and gracious buildings looking out over the water are both admired and desired.

On a hot summer's day, it sometimes seems as though half of Chicago is beside the lake. The energetic will be playing volleyball barefooted in the fine sand but, before July, the water in the lake is cold and really only suitable for the hardy. Beside the cycle and roller-skating track, at a level with Division Street, a branch of **Bike Chicago** offers a range of bikes and skates for rent. If you want to start your cycle tour early at 8am and stay out until 8pm, you should use the Navy Pier branch at 600 E. Grand Avenue. Expert rollerbladers can demonstrate their skills on a concrete track just north of Oak Street.

The **Chess Pavilion** 49, a little further on, provides the boards marked out in the cement, but you will have to supply the pieces and the clock. Volleyball is the main attraction a stone's throw away, and the North Avenue Beach House has changing and showering facilities. At summer weekends, beach volleyball championships often last until well into the evening. Some companies have built fitness and obstacle courses here and anyone can compete for T-shirts, baseball caps and the like.

At the next pedestrian bridge over Lake Shore Drive, you will come to the southern end of pretty **Lincoln Park**, where in the southwest corner the **★★ Chicago Historical Society** 50 has its museum (Monday to Saturday 9.30am–4.30pm, Sunday noon–5pm). You can see the brick building with its classical portico from the bridge, just to the left behind some baseball pitches. To reach it you pass a statue of Franklin and go through an underpass. The museum portrays the city's past and the pioneering era through a collection of everyday objects, artifacts from the Civil War, painstakingly laid-out dioramas, realistic street scenes and a locomotive from the days of the Wild West. Impressive temporary exhibitions complement the permanent displays.

Return along the same route to the Franklin memorial. The avenue that begins here leads to a small lake which is shared by dark gray swans and colorful pedalos. To the left of the South Pond, a small model farm, known as the **Farm in the Zoo** (daily

9am–4.30pm) forms part of the Lincoln Park Zoo complex. It comprises several stables with cows, horses, goats, sheep and pigs. At certain times of the day, jobs such as milking and butter-making are demonstrated.

On the north side of the lake, after an underpass, stands the **Café Brauer**, a building in the typical Prairie House Style of Frank Lloyd Wright with terracing and a landing stage for pedalos. The café serves coffee, cakes and ice cream, plus snacks like pizza, hot dogs and hamburgers. Behind the café, the gates of the ★★ **Lincoln Park Zoo** 🔵 are open all year round (daily 9am–5pm), but cyclists and skaters are not allowed to ride through it. The best thing to do here is to bear left, head to the north end of the zoo and park your bike by the greenhouse.

Lincoln of Lincoln Park

Apart from houses and open spaces for the big cats and large mammals, the zoo also boasts a monkey house and a lagoon for aquatic birds. More than 2,000 animals, including 44 endangered species, entertain about 4 million visitors each year. Walking through Lincoln Park, you'll also encounter the statues of some well-known personalities, including the 100-year-old memorial of Hans Christian Andersen by John Gelert and also one dedicated to the German playwright Schiller by Ernst Rau (1886). Outside the greenhouse a bust of Sir George Solti looks earnestly across at the youthful Schiller.

Sizzling in summer

41

On the other side of Fullerton Parkway at North Pond is the ★★ **Peggy Notebaert Nature Museum of the Chicago Academy of Sciences** 🔵 (Monday, Tuesday, Thursday to Sunday 10am–6pm, 5pm in winter; Wednesday 10am–8pm). This nature museum is the only museum to specialize in the ecology and natural history of the Midwest. Permanent exhibits include Butterfly Haven, City Science, Environmental Central, Water Lab, Wilderness Walk, and the Children's Gallery. The award-winning architecture blends extremely well with the surrounding park, by using lots of glass and different level terraces.

Walking towards the north end of **North Pond** 🔵 you will reach Plum Café, located in a low building near a playground, open mainly during summer weekends. In the park behind it, a gleaming gold statue of Alexander Hamilton is visible through the foliage. In the northwest corner of this section of the park stands a memorial to the celebrated German playwright Goethe, erected in 1913.

Lounging by the lake

Now head eastward towards Lake Michigan. En route you will pass a shaded memorial to a former governor of Illinois, John Peter Altgeld (1847–1902). He is remembered for sacrificing his career for justice, by pardoning the defendants in the Haymarket Square riot on the grounds that no evidence had been presented which actually connected them with the throwing of a bomb. He was not re-elected.

Diversey Harbor is connected to the lake by a narrow channel. From the **North Pier**, where mainly motor boats are moored, you can enjoy a fine view of downtown Chicago's skyline. To the north of the harbor, skirt round the golf driving range to the left, until you reach a children's playground that is level with Barry Avenue. Pass beneath Lake Shore Drive and **Belmont Harbor** ⑤, a yachting marina, lies in front of you.

In 1985 the weather-worn **totem pole**, which had been erected to the north of the harbor by Canadian Indians from the Pacific Coast region, was replaced by a replica. The original pole had been bought from the Indians by the owner of the Kraft food company in 1926 and then donated to the park authorities. Today, the land between the pole and the lake is fenced off as a **bird reserve**.

Continuing northwards, you will pass tennis courts to the left and also a number of baseball pitches. Over to the right on a hill stands a church, which is now used by a golf club. The nine-hole **Sydney R. Marovitz Golf Course** ⑤ is regarded as the best golf course within the city limits. The **Waveland Café** outside serves massive breakfasts and big lunches, and guests will also have the opportunity to watch a sport that is only played in Chicago, namely 'clincher'. This game closely resembles baseball, but nobody wears any gloves and the ball is bigger.

Another yachting marina, **Montrose Harbor** ⑤, is situated by the lakeside.

As you return from **Belmont Avenue** and **Belmont Harbor**, stay beside the lake. The ★ **Theater on the Lake** ⑤, a flat building at the end of Fullerton Parkway, stands on a headland. No theater group is based here, so all the Chicago companies, both dramatic and operatic, use the rather bare stage setting. Most performances begin at around 8pm. For further information, call 312-742-7994/5.

42

Belmont street scene

Bargains along Belmont

Tour 6

South along the lake

Navy Pier – Grant Park – Field Museum of Natural History – Shedd Aquarium – Adler Planetarium – Museum of Science and Industry *See map on page 44*

This second lakeside bike tour may resemble a trip from one museum to another, as this part of Chicago was the site of the World Expositions and many of the grand edifices that were built for those occasions have been converted into museums. Nevertheless, the tour passes through some very relaxing parts of the city and it is nowhere near as crowded as the north side. After Navy Pier, one of the few places on land with a view over the Chicago skyline, comes Grant Park, a vast open space where many open-air events are held. In the summer, it is not only the venue for music concerts of every kind, but also the setting for other traditional festivals such as the boat parade, fireworks on Independence Day and the Taste of Chicago feeding frenzy. If you want to do justice to the next three sights, then allow at least a day for this tour. After a longish section beside the shores of one or two sandy beaches of Lake Michigan, you will discover a fascinating museum where it's possible to spend hours exploring the scientific world with the aid of push-buttons.

From Oak Street Beach (*see Tour 5, page 40*) a path leads south to an artificial headland, where an installation purifies the water from the lake and pumps it on as drinking water. Pipes from four pumping stations converge on the **Jardine Water Purification Plant** ㊽. These pumps, which collect water from the bottom of the lake, are situated some 2 miles (3km) out and are responsible for supplying some 5.1 million people. The plant, the biggest of its kind in the world, can only be visited in groups (for further information, call 312-744-7001).

From the park in front there is good view over downtown Chicago and the same applies to the promenade of the ★★ **Navy Pier** ㊾, a recreational area built on 20,000 wooden piles that extends over half a mile (almost 1km) out into the lake. It was originally built as a landing stage for freighters and pleasure boats, and its function has constantly changed. In 1989, it took on yet another role: now there is a Ferris wheel, an open-air stage for up to 1,500 spectators, a movie theater for 3-D films, the **Chicago Children's Museum** (daily 10am–5pm, Thursday 10am–8pm), a crystal palace with palm trees and a congress center. Restaurants, boutiques, several smaller music stages and street entertainers complete the picture, together with

Entertainers on the pier

43

Navy Pier pumping station

Wheels and thrills

modern sculptures from 175 international galleries. Pleasure boats offer lake and river cruises. Children love the Navy Pier, particularly its fountains at the front entrance.

In an extension towards the city center, another tourist attraction, the ★★ **North Pier 60**, occupies an old warehouse. This pier consists of a shopping center, several restaurants and leisure attractions, as well as an indoor golf course and the ★★ **Bicycle Museum of America** (Monday to Thursday 10am–9pm, Friday and Saturday 10am–10pm, Sunday 11am–6pm). With more than 140 bikes, some over 200 years old, this is one of the biggest bicycle museums in the world.

To the west of Chicago Harbor lies ★★★ **Grant Park**, Chicago's 'front yard'. It is a huge area, where the Petrillo Band Shell frequently serves as a venue for grand musical events. Blues, gospel and country festivals attract thousands of fans, but the free concerts given by the Grant Park Symphony Orchestra are the highlights of the summer season. On special occasions, when, say, Placido Domingo or Santana perform here, families and friends gather early in the afternoon, spread out on the grass to secure a good place and start the musical event with a picnic. Another attraction – a real spectacle in the evenings – is the opulent **Buckingham Fountain**, the biggest fountain in the world. During the summer, about 4 million people come to admire its 20-minute long display. From 9pm in the evening, set against a skyscraper backdrop, a fantastic computer-operated lightshow accompanies the cascades.

Adjoining the southern end of the park is a three-part museum complex: the Field Museum of Natural History, the Shedd Aquarium and the Adler Planetarium. All of them are worth a closer look. The ★★ **Field Museum of Natural History 61** (daily 9am–5pm) was opened in 1921 on a site which the 1909 Burnham Plan had earmarked for a grand civic building. This neo-classical edifice of white marble with Ionic columns is reminiscent of a Greek temple. Originally founded to house the biological and anthropological collections assembled for the World's Columbian Exposition in 1893, it holds more than 20 million specimens of which only a fraction can be exhibited at any one time. Prized displays range from the skeleton of a brontosaurus to the seat of a Pontiac Coupé that was pierced by a meteorite, from the aroma of foreign spices to the fragrance of exotic flowers, from the sound of Caribbean drums to the song of the whale. The museum's exhibition and research programs are further informed by a world-class natural history library of more than 250,000 volumes.

Life underwater is the theme of the ★★★ **Shedd Aquarium** ❻❷, the biggest aquarium in the world (summer, daily 9am–6pm, Thursday until 8pm (oceanarium) or 9pm (aquarium); winter Monday to Friday 9am–5pm, Saturday and Sunday 9am–6pm). The original building centers around a large tank, where shoals of Caribbean fish dart around a coral reef, accompanied by several sharks and a one-eyed tarpon, nicknamed 'Deadeye'. Around 11am and 2pm, a diver feeds the sharks by hand. A further 200 tanks with about 8,000 fish and 650 species contain creatures from all over the world.

Aquarium explorations

A supplement is required for admission to the newer **oceanarium**, the world's largest self-contained pool for sea mammals. Every 90 minutes from 10.30am, the mammals do a performance; spectators can watch the elegant movements of these whales and dolphins and hear their underwater calls.

Before you enter the ★ **Adler Planetarium** ❻❸ (Monday to Thursday 9am–5pm; in summer Monday to Wednesday until 6pm, Thursday until 9pm; Friday 9am–9pm, Saturday and Sunday 9am–6pm), the first planetarium in the western hemisphere, you can consult Henry Moore's sundial to check whether you have enough time to visit. As well as some informative pictures of the night sky, there is also a comprehensive collection of exhibits that date from the early days of astronomy right up to the space age. The planetarium's *tour de force* is a multimedia **Skyshow**, which starts in the Universe Theater on the lowest floor and finishes in the Sky Theater beneath the dome; 150 projectors create the special effects.

45

The Adler is one of America's oldest planetariums

The Field Museum

To the south of the planetarium lies a popular sandy beach with changing cabins and showers, but do not expect to find peace and quiet here on hot, sunny days, as the runway for Meigs Field Airport is nearby and there always seems to be a plane taking off.

Solidarity Drive, named in honor of Lech Walesa, the founder of the Polish Solidarity movement, is lined with a series of monuments dedicated to Polish and Czech celebrities. Copernicus was the founder of modern astronomy (this statue is a copy of one by the classical Danish sculptor, Bertel Thorvaldsen), Havlicek was a Czech poet and the mounted Kosciuzsko, a Polish hero, took part in the American War of Independence.

Soldier Field as seen from the Sears Tower

To the south behind the Field Museum stands another classical-style building, **Soldier Field** ❻❹, a sports arena for the city's football team, the Chicago Bears, with capacity for 106,000 spectators. When the football season ends in January, the stadium is used for open-air festivals, religious conventions and similar events.

The cycleway runs east of the McCormick Place complex further south. **McCormick Place** ❻❺ consists of three vast structures and is one of the biggest convention and exhibition halls in the world. The designer of the east building, Gene R. Summers, worked for 16 years with Mies van der Rohe. What are impressive are the projecting roof structure and the huge exhibition hall, which has only eight supporting pillars. The completion of the south building in 1997 doubled the surface area of the complex.

Narrow **Burnham Park** lies between the lake and stately **Lake Shore Drive**. Cyclists and rollerbladers can press ahead unimpeded to reach the very interesting ★★★ **Museum of Science and Industry** ❻❻ (summer, daily 9.30am–5.30pm, Friday until 9pm; winter Monday to Friday 9.30am–4pm, Saturday and Sunday 9.30am–5.30pm). This museum is one of the only building to survive from the 1893 Columbian Exposition. It was erected as a palace of fine arts and at the end of the exhibition became the forerunner for the Field Museum. During the Depression its future was threatened, but Julius Rosenbaum of Sears & Roebuck donated 5 million dollars towards its conversion into a museum.

Displays from the Museum of Science and Industry

It soon became one of the city's most popular museums, attracting about 3 million visitors per year. Prized displays include a World War II submarine and a reconstruction of a coal mine. Children love this museum for its clear explanations, demonstrations and hands-on exhibits of scientific principles. You can go inside practically everything, including a model of a human heart.

The grand Windermere House opposite is a popular spot for museum visitors to draw breath and enjoy a cup of coffee and a snack Italian-style in the Piccolo Mondo Café.

A round trip through Hyde Park

International House – Robie House – Oriental Institute – Smart Museum

Hyde Park is the cultural center of Chicago's South Side. Around the University of Chicago a small, culturally-mixed intellectual elite live in an oasis of prosperity – their houses were designed by the city's most famous architects. Apart from Robie House in Frank Lloyd Wright's Prairie House Style – now converted into a museum – these buildings can only be seen from outside. Dotted among the wooded residential areas are museums and university institutes. Including the journey there and back and museum visits, this tour should take only half a day.

University of Chicago

To reach Hyde Park by car, follow Lake Shore Drive southwards and park near the Museum of Science and Industry or, as in Tour 6, cycle along the coast and turn off to Hyde Park before the museum. If you want to use public transportation, the CTA's southbound museum bus No.10 from North Michigan Avenue passes all the main museums, terminating at the Museum of Science and Industry. The METRA train from the junction of Michigan Avenue and Randolph Street as far as 59th Street is also convenient. Note: this area is best visited in daylight hours.

47

If you are setting out from the Museum of Science and Industry (*see Tour 6, page 46*), take the opportunity to walk through the park behind the museum. The view of the museum from the bridge on the other side of the lake is similar to that which greeted visitors to the 1893 Columbian Exposition. If starting from the METRA Station on 59th Street, first head west. On the left runs the wide Midway Plaisance corridor, one of the exhibition's main thoroughfares.

Presidential plaque

On the right-hand side lies the extensive **University of Chicago** campus. The university was founded by a professor of Hebrew, William Rainy Harper, a polymath who was a lecturer at the age of 16 and the principal of a college at 19. He managed to persuade John D. Rockefeller, one of the wealthiest men of the time, to part with $600,000. This donation and many others were used to found the college in 1892. No other university in the world has produced so many Nobel Prize winners. An astounding one in six of the students go on to become academics.

The first University of Chicago building is **International House** ⑥⑦, which dates from 1932.

Campus charm

*The college has produced
many Nobel Prize winners*

Detail from an educational edifice

This center, solidly constructed to a design by Holabird & Root, is used as a meeting place and a residence by students and academics from foreign universities. It was the last building to be built in the college's traditional neo-Gothic style. On the first level there is a cafeteria with a shady courtyard that is open to the public.

Pass a few tennis courts and then on your right you will see one of the experimental schools that accepts all age groups from kindergarten level up to high school. These **Laboratory Schools** 🕲 were founded in 1896 by one of the leading figures in the 'progressive' movement in American education, John Dewey (1859–1952), and were run by him until his retirement in 1904. As a great believer in the pragmatic approach to education, Dewey wanted to get away from the traditional curriculum, preferring to place the emphasis on a rounded education, which included the development of manual skills and a serious consideration of the interests and personality of his pupils. He emphasized the maxim 'learning by doing' and also the need for a more understanding relationship between teacher and student. As a supporter of the Hull House neighborhood center, Dewey was interested in helping the socially disadvantaged children of immigrant workers who were welcomed at his Laboratory School. The percentage of pupils from this school who now go on to the best universities in the country is well above average.

The **Ida Noyes Hall** 🕲 is a hive of student activity. There are lounges for students to meet and talk, a library and a theater. Dancing lessons are available and there is also a cinema showing different feature movies each day (Monday to Thursday 7pm, Friday and Saturday 7 and 9.30pm). The Tudor Revival-style building has a hall with a grand 'merrie England' staircase. Meet here for a free hour-long guided tour of the campus.

The **Rockefeller Memorial Chapel** ❼⓿ is dedicated to the college's first sponsor and the main events in the university's calendar are enacted here: concerts, special performances and the graduation ceremony (concerts: Wednesday 12.15pm when the students are on campus, Thursday 7.30pm, Sunday 4pm during the months of June, July and August). This neo-Gothic building was designed by the architect of New York's Empire State Building, Bertram G. Goodhue. He is immortalized by a statue in the transept, representing architecture in the same way that Bach, opposite, represents music. The tower holds the second biggest carillon in the world – it has a range of six octaves. On the death of a woman, the death knell sounds six times, for a man nine times. When a famous personality dies, the biggest bell tolls again with one strike for every year of his or her life.

Robie House is open to the public

Woodlawn Avenue runs between the last two buildings straight to the ★★ **Frederick C. Robie House** ❼❶ (guided tours at noon), one of the most important residential houses ever designed in the US. Designed by Frank Lloyd Wright in 1909, it was paraded as an example of the Prairie House Style. The point where the two 2-story wings converge is dominated by a square third story, but the house does not lose its horizontal alignment. All the rooms are grouped around the chimney, which acts as a focal point. Robie House is open to the public and you can explore the interior and admire the built-in closets, the leaded windows and the spacious kitchen.

49

Oriental Institute artifacts

Head westward from Robie House to the ★ **Oriental Institute** ❼❷, which exhibits finds that teams from the institute brought back from expeditions and excavations carried out in the Near East. The building opposite is the **Chicago Theological Seminary**.

Further west lies the ★★ **University of Chicago Quadrangle** ❼❸, which is surrounded by buildings on three sides. The design and layout of the quad clearly draws inspiration from its medieval English counterparts in Oxford and Cambridge. Apart from the three modern constructions, the 34 buildings follow a neo-Gothic style and they combine to create a unified impression. Shaded in summer by grand, old trees, the spaces between the buildings form an oasis of tranquility. The café on the second level in the Classics Building in the southwest corner has a Gothic window facade and, from the mantelpiece behind the bar, a blue Socrates stares down at your drink.

The administrative block is situated in the west by a circular flower-bed. Behind it to the left stands the university hospital complex which takes up two blocks. On the right-hand side in a building dating from 1902 is the **Barnes & Noble** university bookstore, plus café.

A little further to the west, the **Cummings Life Science**

Henry Moore's 'Nuclear Energy'

Court Theater

Future scholars take a stroll

Center **74** rises up like a modern fortress. It is the tallest building in the university and is topped with modern battlements. The architects who were commissioned to work on this extension of the university in the post-war years sought to create something which blended in with the original neo-Gothic design, if only in an abstract sense. Public feeling seems to be that they succeeded.

The **Enrico Fermi Institute** in Ellis Avenue on the left and Henry Moore's 12-ton sculpture *Nuclear Energy* **75** one block further on to the right both serve as reminders of the first controled nuclear chain reaction. This momentous event took place on December 2, 1942 under the leadership of the Nobel Prize-winner Enrico Fermi in a squash court beneath a sports stand. People spoke of Fermi's 'suicide squad', because none of the scientists involved could be sure what was going to happen. This event marked the first stage in the creation of the atomic bomb and also the peaceful use of nuclear energy. Moore's sculpture is sometimes referred to as the 'Skull'.

On the right-hand side to the north, the next complex comprises the Court Theater and the David and Alfred Smart Museum of Art. The **Court Theater** **76** has space for an audience of 250 and its season lasts from September to May. Included in its repertoire are great European dramas such as Molière's *Tartuffe* and Bizet's *Carmen* as well as famous modern classics.

The ★★ **Smart Museum** **77** (Tuesday to Friday 10am–4pm, Saturday and Sunday noon–6pm) has an unusual collection of exhibits and will certainly provide some surprises. It covers 5,000 years of history and its permanent display includes ancient Greek vases and Chinese bronzes, ceramics by contemporary potters, paintings by old masters, furniture and windows from Robie House designed by Frank Lloyd Wright and quite a few modern sculptures, from Rodin to Moore.

Other treasures include photographs by Walker Evans and Ansel Adams, prints by Albrecht Dürer and Rembrandt and drawings by Georg Grosz and Henry Moore. In addition, every year the museum organizes excellent special exhibitions, lectures, guided tours and educational courses for young children. The museum café has tables outside and serves coffee, snacks and cake (Monday to Friday 9am–4pm, Saturday and Saturday noon–5pm).

To conclude the walk, proceed westward along **57th Street**, where there are a number of second-hand bookstores and two or three popular bars.

On the journey back to the METRA station, look out for the houses along **Harper Avenue** – some were designed by Solon S. Beman, the architect of the Pullman project. They embody the notion of a rural idyll that permeates the Hyde Park district.

Tour 8

Homage in Oak Park

On the trail of Frank Lloyd Wright

**Unity Temple – Ernest Hemingway Museum – Frank
Lloyd Wright Home and Studio** *See map on page 53*

Oak Park is associated with two famous men. One, Ernest
Hemingway, never bothered much about his birthplace
– although there are two small museums dedicated to him,
open only at weekends (Friday to Sunday). The other
celebrity, Frank Lloyd Wright, later enhanced the district
with his works and now, thanks to his fame, has endowed
the neighborhood with an almost museum-like status. If
you want to escape the hectic bustle of downtown Chicago,
then the sights of Oak Park provide a relaxing alternative as you trace the development of the Prairie House
Style from its early days. Thirty Frank Lloyd Wright buildings still survive here and fans can borrow an informative Walkman cassette from the Visitors Center near Unity
Temple. The residences are still named after their initial
owners and, as they are in private hands, can only be
viewed from outside.

Frank Lloyd Wright, 1895

To reach Oak Park by car, leave the Eisenhower Expressway at the Harlem Avenue exit and then turn off to
the north (right). After an underpass on Lake Street, turn
right to the Visitors Center, where there is a car park. Alter-
natively, Oak Park can be reached from the city center
by the new Green Line train. Leave the Loop and head
in a straight line to the terminus at Harlem.

When you arrive on the El, follow South Boulevard
eastward as far as Marion Street, then pass under the railroad track and head northwards. The map of the district
at the entrance to the pedestrianized zone will help you

Frank W. Thomas House

Charles E. Matthews House

Unity Temple

to find your bearings. If you are already in need of a rest, there are two cafés with shaded seats outside in the small shopping street. The **Visitors Center** ⓻ in Forest Avenue (Monday to Friday 10am–5pm) provides maps, tour information and cassettes. Almost directly behind, at 210 Forest, is the low-slung **Frank W. Thomas House**, which gives a taste of what is to come. Just north, and one block away at 432 N. Kenilworth, is the **Charles E. Matthews House**, built in 1909.

East on the corner of Lake Street and Kenilworth Avenue, partly hidden away behind trees, is Frank Lloyd Wright's ★★★ **Unity Temple** ⓽ (Monday to Friday 10am–5pm; guided tours on Saturday and Sunday at 1, 2 and 3pm). This church, completed in 1905, is one of only two buildings in Prairie House Style in Oak Park that is open to the public – and it is still being used for its original function. The architect regarded this temple, which had to be built within an extremely tight budget, as 'the true embodiment of my idea that the space inside a building should represent the reality of that building'.

Even before you enter, you are shielded from the outside world. As well as the obvious features of the Prairie House Style, there is a new concept in ornamentation, both inside and out. With rich amber light flooding the interior, the window design here was one of Wright's most impressive achievements. The congregation in the gallery are taken as close as possible to the preacher and they leave by going towards him, not away from him.

Further east along Lake Street lies the rich green grounds of **Scoville Park**. Here a Wright-designed concrete fountain stands in the southeast corner and a memorial in the center displays the name of Hemingway as a participant in World War I. A museum has been established to honor the famous writer in a former Christian Scientist church. The ★★ **Ernest Hemingway Museum** ⓾ (Wednesday, Friday and Sunday 1–5pm, Saturday 10am–5pm) is located on the other side of the park on the corner of Oak Park Avenue and Ontario Street. In the museum, manuscripts, letters, photographs, books, movie posters, personal objects, quotations and a life-sized military scene document the author's life. One short video summarizes his school years, others are devoted to his life and his work. Hemingway fans can also watch, one after the other, all the Hollywood movies that were adapted from his novels and short stories.

Just one block further in N. Euclid Street (No. 223) stands the **George W. Furbeck House** ⓷⓵, dating from 1897. Here, Wright deceives the passer-by with an optical illusion: the rooms on the first floor appear to be taller than those on the upper floor. The original design has, unfortunately, been altered in the entrance hall area.

The **Charles E. Roberts House** ➋ (321 N. Euclid) and the former stables that have been converted into a house was actually designed by Burnham & Root in 1883, but Wright was responsible for redesigning the interior 13 years later. The owner at that time was an early supporter of Wright and was partly instrumental in securing for him the Unity Temple contract.

In Oak Park Avenue (No. 339) is **Ernest Hemingway's birthplace** ➌. Carefully restored to its original condition, the house contains exhibits which illustrate the culturally-enriched day-to-day life of the three generations that lived under this roof. Grace, Ernest's mother, gave up a career as an opera singer at the Met and was keen to develop the children's musical education. But for Ernest, his upbringing was too provincial and he is said to have remarked that in Oak Park the 'lawns are wide but the minds small' (same opening times as museum).

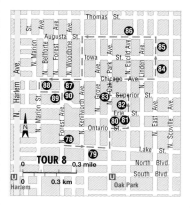

At this point, architecture buffs may like to take a small detour northwards along Chicago Avenue and eastward as far as East Avenue. The single-story ★★ **Edwin H. Cheney House** ➍ (520 North East Avenue) alone is worth the effort. It is a typical Frank Lloyd Wright Prairie House Style building which has striking similarities with the Robie House in Hyde Park (*see Tour 7, page 49*). The building of the house marked the beginning of the end of Wright's involvement with Chicago. While working on the project, he met and immediately fell in love with Edwin Cheney's wife, Mamah. Cheney and Wright remained friends, but Wright's long-suffering wife, Catherine, who had borne him six children, could not come to terms with her husband's infidelity.

The Wright stuff

Wright and his wife separated and the two lovers finally moved away to settle in Taliesin in Spring Green, Wisconsin. But their relationship was to be abruptly ended. In 1914 a crazed former employee set fire to their home and beat to death with an axe anyone who tried to leave. Within a matter of minutes, seven people, including Mamah and the two children from her first marriage, were dead. Wright himself, heartbroken but resolute, lived for many more years, and only died in 1959. The **William E. Martin House** ➎, in the same street (No. 636), is another building in mature Prairie style. Its outward opening casement windows bring a feeling of width to the room and its height is minimized by the emphasis on horizontal lines.

The last building that Wright designed in Oak Park is the **Henry S. Adams House** ➏ at 710 W. Augusta Street. A spacious house dating from 1913, its sheltered entrance portal is a typical Wrightian feature.

Details, FLW's home and studio

Nathan G. Moore House

Arthur B. Heurtley House

Evenutally, it is possible to explore the interior of a house designed by Wright, but only as part of a guided tour. The ★★ **Frank Lloyd Wright Home and Studio** ❸ (tours Monday to Friday at 11am, 1 and 3pm, Saturday and Sunday 11am–4pm), at 951 Chicago Avenue, was where the architect settled with his wife and family in 1898. It was here that he developed his inimitable Prairie House Style. The National Trust has had to carry out some extensive restoration work, but the premises are more or less as they were when Wright and his wife separated in 1909. The home is dominated by a bold pitched-roof second floor, an equilateral triangle pierced by diamond-pane windows set in rectangular array. Of special interest inside are the ornamentation and the furniture that Wright himself designed. He even designed clothes for his wife to match the interior decor.

A little further west along Chicago Avenue (nos. 1019/1027/1031), three of Wright's earlier creations still remain. They caused a rift between himself and Louis Sullivan, his boss at the time, that lasted until just before the latter's death. Wright, desperately short of money, worked on them behind Sullivan's back in breach of his contract. This explains why these homes were called ★★ **Bootleg Homes** ❽. They all bear a resemblance to one another and also to **Furbeck House** of pre-Prairie vintage.

The imposing ★ **Nathan G. Moore House** ❽ at the southwest corner of Superior Street and Forest Avenue is the result of a compromise between the owner and the architect. The owner wanted a house in Tudor style, but Wright was not keen on that design, so he included some unusual decorative features: the mixture of Gothic, Japanese, Sullivan-inspired and Mayan ornaments (which fascinated the architect) blended so well with a building with a steeply pointed roof that Wright once remarked that he could have had enough contracts for that design to keep him going for the rest of his life. The owner was happy too. When the top floor burned down in 1922, he reengaged Wright as the architect.

With its distinctive external features, the **Arthur B. Heurtley House** ❾, opposite the Nathan G. Moore house, is another typical example of the Prairie design: it has a projecting, gently sloping roof with the horizontal line emphasized by the texture of the rows of bricks. There is also a circular entrance with an arch highlighted by a broad band and ornamented, mainly lead-glazed windows. The windows give the residents a respite from the prying eyes of Wright fans and allows a mellow light to flood the room.

And that brings you back to the Visitors Center at the southern end of Forest Avenue. If you have acquired an appetite after your exertions, there are a number of good restaurants in **Marion Street**.

Tour 9

The southern suburbs

Pullman – Chinatown – Pilsen *See backcover map and CTA map on page 82*

Chicago consists of no less than 77 districts, each with its own distinctive identity. These residential districts, or neighborhoods, provide a fascinating insight into the city's social as well as ethnic development.

A special chapter in Chicago's history was written at the beginning of the century in Pullman in the south of the city. The luxury railroad car manufacturer set up a model workers' village, where the company owned everything. The settlement remains today and it is interesting to take a stroll through this piece of social history.

On the journey back to the city from Pullman, stop off in Chinatown. While it cannot match the Chinese quarters of New York or San Francisco for size or color, it nevertheless has an important place in Chicago's multi-cultural melting pot and is well worth a visit.

Chinatown today

Pilsen is nearby and, as the name suggests, the immigrants who arrived in this quarter at the turn of the century came mainly from Bohemia. Many of the buildings still show evidence of their past, even though the inhabitants today are mainly of Mexican origin.

A day is required to make the most of this tour. All three districts are easy to reach with public transportation.

Pullman

For Pullman, obtain a transfer ticket for a token, plus a few cents, take the CTA Red Line southwards (to Dan Ryan) and travel as far as the terminus on 95th Street. Use the

Pullman around 1900

A model community

Named after Pullman's daughter

transfer ticket to board bus No. 104 or No. 111 and get off at 111th Street. The Hotel Florence should now be visible in the southeast. To reach Pullman by car, stay on the Dan Ryan Expressway (Interstate 94) until just after 95th Street, merge into the Calumet Expressway (now Interstate 94) there and then by 111th Street turn off to the west. You can park outside the Hotel Florence, the starting point for this short tour.

On the first Sunday in the month (from May to October), you can join an official guide through Pullman. It starts at the **Visitor Center** on the other side of the hotel parking lot at 12.30 or 1.30pm.

George M. Pullman (1831–97) arrived in Chicago in 1855 as a cabinet-maker and construction engineer. He quickly earned a reputation as a reliable engineer, when he organized the raising of many buildings from the marshy soil. Having realized that there would be travelers willing to pay for the extra comfort, he then turned his hand to the design of a luxury sleeper car for use on the transcontinental railroads. The development of lounge cars and restaurant cars followed, and in 1867 he founded his own company, The Pullman Palace Car Company. His factory in southern Chicago was opened in 1880. Keen that his staff should give their best to the company, he built a town with 1,800 dwellings around the factory. Pullman was a model industrial town where the company owned everything. Workers were housed in tidy homes on streets that were paved and landscaped by the company. The company set the rents and controled prices at its local stores. Alcohol, trade unions and anything else the company boss regarded as immoral, were banned.

Many regarded Pullman as a near-Utopian village. But during the recession of 1893, one third of all workers were laid off and the remainder had their wages cut by 30 to 40 percent. When the workers demanded a corresponding rent reduction, the magnate was dumbstruck. A strike followed in 1894, but Pullman stood firm. After violent exchanges between workers and the police, federal troops were called on to move against the workers. The strike collapsed, but only after 30 workers were shot. Pullman's victory was shortlived, however. In 1898 the company lost the right to own the factory site and by 1907 Pullman had sold all his houses to the occupants or other interested parties. It was never the same. The last Pullman car was manufactured in 1981.

The ★ **Hotel Florence**, now a sort of museum, was named after Pullman's favorite daughter. Here you can buy a map of Pullman and join a short guided tour through the hotel. If you want a meal in its restaurant after touring the district, then be sure to book a table in advance. Hotel Florence contains the factory owner's suites and items of pre-1900 furniture. Years ago the authorities promised to restore the building to its former glory and to re-open it as a hotel, but funding remains a problem.

To the east of 111th Street stand Pullman's fine **residences**. Here lived the factory manager and the company doctor, Dr John McLean, a friend of the boss. **Retreat**, a French-American restaurant, now occupies the carefully restored home of the company's first dean.

Turn off 111th Street into Champlain and you will pass the workers' houses before reaching the **Market Hall**. Having been damaged by fire on a number of occasions, only the first floor remains. The square is surrounded by Italian-style colonnades and the adjoining dwellings were used as accommodation by visitors to the 1893 Columbian Exposition. Apprentices lived in the rooms above.

Follow 112th Street eastward and in Langley you will discover houses that were originally used by the workers on the lowest rung of the hierarchical ladder. Located further south in Champlain were the so-called **Honeymoon Cottages** for newly-weds.

Today the **Historic Pullman Center** in 113th Street between Champlain and St Lawrence serves as a community center, where matters of concern to the residents are discussed and educational courses are held.

The company's skilled workers tended to live in the **St Lawrence houses** to the north. They could enjoy an open fireplace with marble facing and three upstairs bedrooms. Further north is Pullman's **old hospital**, now converted into homes. At the end of the street stands what must be, after the Hotel Florence, the most spectacular building in the town, the ★ **Greenstone Church**. The green stone originates from a quarry in Pennsylvania and is the only significant building material that Pullman brought in from far afield. Although the church was originally intended to serve all faiths, the United Methodist Church now holds its services here.

Guided tours of Pullman take place monthly

Greenstone Church

Diagonally opposite the church lie the remains of once-beautiful **Arcade Park**. The houses on the east and west sides are among the better equipped houses; their facades were meant to enhance the appearance of the park and they were set aside for the school principal, foremen and other workers who could afford to pay higher rents.

The **stables** opposite the Visitor Center are now used by automobile repair companies. Carvings of horses' heads on the facade serve as reminders of the original occupants. Horses were not actually welcomed by the parsimonious Mr Pullman. The stables were there only for the convenience of visitors and horses were not allowed on to the streets as this meant extra work for the road sweepers.

White Sox Park

Head back to the north by bus and El or by car. On the way, you will pass the Robert Taylor Homes on the right and the new White Sox stadium on the left. The **Taylor Homes** scheme was the biggest national social housing project in the world and many believe it was a catastrophe of indescribable proportions. Some 28 identical 16-story blocks comprising 4,300 apartments were built to accommodate low-income families. Living conditions in this district, which rapidly became a ghetto, are characterized by unemployment, poverty, neglect, crime and drugs. The police, fire-brigade and emergency services leave the inhabitants largely to themselves and tourists should give this district a wide berth at all times of day.

The new **White Sox Park** (1991) replaced a stadium steeped in tradition, so the club's first task was to convince its conservative fans that the move was for the good. Computer simulations ensured that no-one's view was impeded. The new stadium has seating for over 40,000 spectators, four times more than Wrigley Field, the old-style baseball park where the Cubs still play.

Chinatown

If you are using the El, get off at the Cermak Road/Chinatown stop and head westward along Cermak Road as far as Wentworth Avenue. Car drivers should not stay on the Dan Ryan Expressway after 31st Street, but weave their way off it, carry straight on and then turn to the west along Cermak Road, finally parking near Wentworth Avenue.

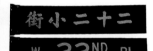

East meets West

Chinatown is really just the triangular district southeast of the southern arm of the Chicago River, bordered by an Expressway in the south and the El in the east. The first Chinese quarter was situated in the South Loop, but in 1912 it had to make way for redevelopment. **Wentworth Avenue** is where visitors will spot the first signs of an

Asian culture. A large red wooden gate marks the start of the area and then just past it on the right stands the most impressive building in the district, the **Pui Tak Center**. This houses the association of Chinese traders, which sees its main functions as helping with the integration of new arrivals and the preservation of the Chinese language and culture. The Chicago architects Michaelsen & Rognstad supplied the owners with the required Oriental flamboyance to the exterior. Note the subtly tinted terracotta facings decorated with Chinese motifs.

Gateway to little Asia

Some of the houses in this street and along the side streets in particular were originally built as simple, central European- or Italian-inspired, immigrant homes. Subsequent decorative work has an American-Chinese finish, a rather bizarre mixture of styles. The modern buildings, on the other hand, bear a strong resemblance to present-day Hong Kong. The small stores sell every kind of Chinese miscellany, and you can titillate your palate in one of the many Chinese restaurants. *Dim sum* is served from noon to about 3pm in the **Three Happiness**.

Kidding around,
Chinese style

Pilsen

The next destination is the neighboring community of **Pilsen**. Follow Cermak Road west as far as Halsted Street. Here, you can catch bus No. 21 or you can go on foot and study at close quarters Chicago's industrial past. You pass beneath the railroad and the Expressway and cross a bascule bridge (1906), almost a museum piece in itself. Old warehouses, factory buildings and abandoned industrial sites eventually give way to a residential district.

59

Pilsen's small **artists' colony** is concentrated around Halsted Street and 18th Street. On a summer weekend, they can often be seen entertaining friends in the rear courtyards of the houses between 18th and 19th Street.

What makes Pilsen so unusual, however, is its complete transformation into a Mexican-dominated area. Follow 18th Street westward and by May Street it will be clear precisely what changes have taken place. The restaurants and bars offer Mexican food and drinks. Churches, where Bohemian, Polish and Lithuanian immigrants once prayed, have been redesigned and now have Mexican murals with motifs that hark back to pre-Columbian cultures.

Pilsen has a number of beer and tequila bars, where the sounds of both *mariachi* and modern music can be heard. If you are hungry, then you will find no shortage of small restaurants selling traditional Mexican fare.

Returning to the city via the El station on the Blue Line (18th Street), it is impossible to avoid more Mexican mythology in the form of a series of wall paintings, many of which illustrate the special relationship devout Mexicans have with death.

Architecture

A Phoenix rises from the ashes

In 1871, Chicago fell victim to one of the biggest urban fires in world history. In barely two days, 300 people lost their lives, 100,000 were rendered homeless, 18,000 buildings were destroyed and the central area of Chicago was reduced to a pile of smoldering ruins. This devastating fire led to the renaissance of modern Chicago, spawning a building boom which attracted the nation's best architects. Larger and more impressive buildings were called for. Techniques used in the construction of large warehouses and by Gustave Eiffel in Europe were applied to the basic structure of all the new buildings. William Le Baron Jenney built the first skyscraper, the Home Insurance Building, around a steel frame. Taller edifices soon followed. But the unadorned functionalism of the early years often failed to satisfy the aesthetic sensitivities of the architects and their clients. The Fisher Building, for example, is less modern-looking than the older Monadnock, exhibiting a nostalgia for old-fashioned forms with an ornamented facade designed to disguise the swarthy steel construction beneath.

Louis H. Sullivan (1856–1924), who had studied in Paris, insisted that the skyscraper should, like its antecedent the Gothic cathedral, have a new face that matched the new era. Furthermore, he sought an original American form for it – and the Carson Pirie Scott building bears witness to both these aspirations. Exuberant ornamentation reminiscent of Art Nouveau can be seen inside; his famous theme 'Form follows Function' is clearly illustrated here.

One of Sullivan's younger colleagues, Frank Lloyd Wright (1867–1959), created a new style, which had a unique American flavor to it: the Prairie House Style. For him, the organic relationship with the landscape played an important part. The many homes that he built in the Chicago area stress the natural horizontal plane and merge in perfectly with the gentle rhythms of the prairies. In the suburbs of Oak Park and River Forest, the homes are almost museum pieces but, at the same time, also a living testimony to his work.

Mies van der Rohe (1886–1969) brought the Bauhaus principles and the 'International Style' to Chicago in 1938. With his motto 'Less is more', he left the stamp of pure form on American architecture. His steel and glass boxes dispense entirely with ornamentation, corresponding perfectly with Mayor Daley's theme for Chicago as the 'city that works'. Minimalist elegance is expressed at the Federal Center in the Loop. Much of what was subsequently built in Chicago followed van der Rohe's principles.

Opposite: the Picasso Sculpture in Daley Plaza

The Great Fire of 1871 spawned a building boom

Frank Lloyd Wright created a unique American style

Light but tough materials revolutionized skyscrapers

Diagonal steel beams to outer walls add strength

How do skyscrapers reach the sky?

Skyscrapers can reach such heights today because new materials changed the rules. One of the most important advances was the rejection of the walled, load-bearing exterior. In its place, a skeleton, initially made of cast-iron, was encased in a fireproof mantle with no load-bearing role. The introduction of the Bessemer process and mass-produced high-quality steel revolutionized the process of building skyscrapers. Now that a lighter but tougher material was available, not only could the designers build higher, but there was no need for massive supporting walls at the foot of the structure. It became possible to have windows at ground level – an important consideration as stores could occupy the lower floors, while the space above could be adapted to suit corporate requirements.

With no solid walls to incorporate into the structure, architects could apply their creativity to designing the curtain walls, using a whole variety of materials for the purpose, including glass, aluminum, light alloys and ceramics. One of Chicago's most celebrated modern architects, Helmut Jahn, said that he 'decorated structures'.

Despite the use of lighter materials, the foundations of a skscraper still have to carry a phenomenal weight and now usually incorporate several pontoon-style plinths or reinforced concrete pillars driven deep into the ground. The height of a building ultimately depends on the development of better foundations, although the structure above them also has to withstand enormous pressures. Experts believe that with high-performance reinforced concrete it is possible to build to a height of 1 mile (1,600m). Ongoing research suggests that when certain synthetic polymers are added to the usual mix of sand, shingle, water and cement, there will, in theory, be no restrictions on the height of a building. John Norris of Toronto believes that the 'sky is literally the limit'.

Wind pressure is the only other significant problem that tall buildings face, but it is the stability of the building materials which matters here. One solution has been to incorporate diagonal steel beams into the walls and ceilings – clearly visible on the John Hancock Center. The Sears Tower essentially consists of a number of upright blocks which support each other, the lower blocks serving as buttresses to strengthen the tallest block. As the whole tower rises, the surface area exposed to wind currents diminishes. Other solutions are the incorporation of flexible cushions which absorb the vibrations or which adjust automatically in accordance with the wind pressure to maintain equilibrium. The solution which was employed on the Sears Tower seems to have the best prospects. When skyscrapers are 'bundled together', costs are considerably cheaper too.

Music and the Movies

Jazz and blues – the legend lives on

Jazz may not have had its roots in Chicago, but many say it grew up here. With the closure of Storyville, the New Orleans Red Light area, towards the end of World War I, many bands left and moved to Chicago, including King Oliver. Oliver engaged Louis Armstrong (1901–71) as a trumpeter and nurtured him and his new music to world fame. 'Satchmo's' performances drew the masses into the ballrooms and bars. Musicians – both black and white – set out to copy his style. By imitating the New Orleans bands and by emphasizing the soloists' improvisations, the Chicago style of the 1920s emerged. Bix Beiderbecke (1903–31), a white cornetist and a great admirer of Armstrong, became the first cult figure in the annals of jazz when he died prematurely – even though his music was much more inward looking than the master's. During the 1930s, many musicians moved to New York, but Chicago continues to be the spiritual home for many jazz artists. The same is even more true about the blues. It developed among the blacks in the rural South, then moved to the big cities in the North, mainly Chicago. As well as the eternal theme of love, the blues expressed the anguish of the new urban dwellers, who were the losers in this increasingly competitive society. Muddy Waters, Howling Wolf and many others continued the tradition after World War II. It is still likely even today that in one of the many bars, suddenly a mature black female singer will climb on to the stage and demonstrate to the audience what is meant by the blues. The legend lives on.

Local bluesman Magic Slim

63

Chicago in the movies

Chicago's violent history and the telegenic urban backdrop continues to entice Hollywood's film-makers to the city – it should not be forgotten that Hollywood has its roots in Chicago. *The Great Train Robbery*, the first Western in movie history, was made here in 1903. William M. Selig built America's first movie studio south of the Loop in 1897, but in 1907 left for Hollywood as the weather in Chicago was too unreliable. In 1915 Charlie Chaplin earned $1,250 per week while working in Chicago's Essanay Studios. James Cagney, Edward G. Robinson and Humphrey Bogart may have worked in Hollywood, but they brought Chicago's gangsters to the attention of the world. The list of movies that were set in Chicago goes on and on. Here is just a short selection: *The Front Page* (1931), *Scarface* (1932), *The Sting* (1973), *The Blues Brothers* (1980), *The Color of Money* (1986), *The Untouchables* (1987), *Wayne's World* (1991), *The Fugitive* (1993) and *Twilight* (1996).

The Sting

The Blues Brothers

Events calendar

The Boat Show, January

Every summer, various groups have their own carnivals or 'Rock around the Block' parties. Usually a road will be blocked off and a bandstand erected at either end with any number of snack bars and market stalls in between. If you want to know what is going on, then get hold of a copy of *Reader*, a freesheet in which the forthcoming week's events are listed in full. It is available at all bookstores, supermarkets and concert halls.

Early- to mid-January: Chicago Boat, Sports and RV Show. One of Chicago's largest public expositions.

End of January/beginning of February: Chinese New Year Parade along Wentworth Avenue in Chinatown.

Flower and Garden Show, March

Second week in March: Chicago Flower and Garden Show in the Navy Pier's Festival Hall.

March 17: On St Patrick's Day, the Chicago River is colored green. Two parades take place on the nearest weekend: on the Saturday along Dearborn Street between Wacker Drive and Van Buren Street and on the Sunday in Western Avenue between 103rd and 114th Street.

End of March to the beginning of June: Spring Festival of Dance with mainly Chicago dance groups in the Shubert Theater and other venues.

Second week in May: The annual 'Art Chicago' in the Navy Pier's Festival Hall. Exhibition of contemporary art.

Last weekend in May: Viva! Chicago Latin Music Festival, Petrillo Music Shell, Grant Park. In the afternoon and evening.

First weekend in June: Chicago Blues Festival, Petrillo Music Shell, Grant Park. In the afternoon and evening.

Music festivals June to August

Second week in June: Chicago Gospel Festival, Petrillo Music Shell, Grant Park. In the afternoon and evening. The Old Town Art Fair, the oldest art fair in Chicago. Lincoln Park West and New Orleans Street.

Mid-June to mid-August: Grant Park Music Festival, predominantly classical music. In the evening.

Last weekend in June: Chicago Country Music Festival, Petrillo Music Shell, Grant Park. In the afternoon and through the evening.

Last Sunday in June: Gay & Lesbian Pride Parade with a carnival-style procession, starting from Halsted Street and Belmont Avenue, through Lakeview to Lincoln Park.

Street fairs are held throughout the summer

End of June to mid-July: Taste of Chicago, a 10-day feeding frenzy with over 60 food stands from Chicago restaurants.

Taste of Chicago, July

65

Three weekends from mid-July to the beginning of August: University of Chicago Summer Opera Festival on the university campus.

Last Saturday in July: Venetian Night with a procession of boats past Grant Park.

Mid-August: Gold Coast Art Fair, River North; Jazz, Blues and Gospel Festival, an open-air event in North Pullman District; Wicker Park Greening Festival, a large festival in Wicker Park.

Third weekend in August: Chicago Air & Water Show by North Avenue Beach. Boat parade and fly-past.

German festival, September

End of August/beginning of September: Chicago Jazz Festival, Petrillo Music Shell, Grant Park. Afternoon and through the evening.

Mid-September: The Berghoff Oktoberfest. Street festival outside the famous German restaurant.

Middle to end of October: Chicago International Film Festival. Various theaters.

Middle to end of November: Magnificent Mile Lights Festival on N. Michigan Avenue and side streets.

Food and Drink

If you ask what the typical Chicagoan eats, then you will probably get the answer hot dog and pizza. Hot dogs and beer go with the baseball game in the same way that hamburgers, steak and ribs go with the barbecue. The people of Chicago claim to have re-invented the pizza. They talk about the 'deep dish pizza', which has a thick layer of dough and is served in a kind of frying pan. 'Pizzeria Uno' and its sister company 'Due' claim to be the inventors. Although immensely popular, it is not representative of Chicago's gastronomic repertoire. The city boasts over 6,000 restaurants, which serve cuisine from all over the world – ranging from basic snack bars to high-class gourmet haunts.

To gain an insight into the diverse nature of what Chicago can offer, visit the 'Taste of Chicago', a 10-day open-air festival where some 60 of Chicago's restaurants offer samples of their most popular dishes. Dedicated diners swear by *Zagat*, an annual guide which assesses 600 city restaurants. Similarly, the *Official Chicago Bar Guide* appraises 350 different pubs, bars and taverns.

Hispanic food to go

Beer lovers begin here **67**

Everyone in Chicago loves coffee

If you had come to Chicago in the 1980s, you would have found just a handful of continental-style cafés – the term cappuccino was only understood by the Italian community. In fact, to drink anything other than 'regular coffee' was almost frowned upon. However, at the start of the 1990s, Starbucks, a coffee house chain based in Seattle suddenly appeared on the scene. The cafés where various new aromatic brews were served proved very popular. Another chain from Seattle followed and soon the smaller companies were jumping on the bandwagon. Some conservatives were unhappy about the changes. 'This is not San Francisco,' they complained wearily and repeatedly. But times had changed. The service sector had grown dramatically in Chicago, the 'city of broad shoulders', and tastes had altered.

Starbucks started a trend

That something like a 'coffee house culture' emerged is evident in large bookstores like Barnes and Noble or Borders, where the adjoining cafés are clearly flourishing. You can take the book that everyone is talking about from the shelf, order your favorite blend of coffee and settle down at a table to enjoy an undisturbed browse before deciding whether to buy. At the next table, budding Hemingways sit with their laptops (or more traditionally, their notepads) and draft out the next century's bestsellers. In these bookstores and many other cafés, writers give readings, and readers' groups regularly meet to discuss the classics and new publications.

Restaurant selection

The following suggestions are listed according to three categories: $$$ = expensive (from $55); $$ = moderate ($25-$55); $ = inexpensive (up to $25).

Three of the best restaurants

Everest, 440 LaSalle Street, on the 40th floor, tel: 312-663-8920. Tuesday to Thursday 5.30–9pm, Friday and Saturday 5.30–10pm. Excellent French cuisine with a view of night-time Chicago. Seven-course menu. $$$
Topolobampo, 445 N. Clark Street, tel: 312-661-1434. Lunch: Tuesday to Saturday 10.30am–2.30pm, dinner: Tuesday to Thursday 5.30–10pm, Friday and Saturday 5.30–11pm. Regional Mexican cuisine. $$$
Charlie Trotter's, 816 W. Armitage, tel: 773-248-6228. Tuesday to Saturday 5.30pm–midnight. Multi-cultural cuisine always on the look-out for new combinations. $$$

Portions are enormous

The Loop

Russian Tea Time, 77 E. Adams Street, tel: 312-360-0000. Monday 11am–9pm, Tuesday to Thursday 11am–11pm, Friday 11am–midnight, Saturday noon–midnight, Sunday noon–9pm. Lunch reservations for more than four are advisable, for dinner essential. $$
Caffé Baci, 77 W. Wacker Drive, tel: 312-629-2225. Monday to Friday 6.30am–8pm. New Italian cuisine. $$

Great value at The Berghoff

The Berghoff, 17 W. Adams Street, tel: 312-427-3170. Monday to Thursday 11am–9.30pm, Friday and Saturday 11am–10pm. Great-value German-American dishes. $
Ceres Café, in the Chicago Board of Trade Building, tel: 312-427-3443. Monday to Friday 5.30am–8pm. Specials, usually including a fish and pasta, change daily. $
Cellers Market, in the basement of the Board of Trade Building, tel: 312-427-9833. Monday to Friday 6am–2.45pm. Breakfast served until 10.50am. Home-made dishes for 3,500 people every weekday. $

South of the Loop

Gourmand, 728 S. Dearborn, tel: 312-427-2610. Monday to Thursday 7am–11pm, Friday 7am–midnight, Saturday 8am–midnight, Sunday 8am–11pm. Mainly cold dishes like couscous or salads with good bread. $
Blackie's, 755 S. Clark Street, tel: 312-786-1161. Monday and Tuesday 11am–3pm, Wednesday and Thursday 11am–10pm, Friday 7.30am–10pm, Saturday and Sunday 7.30am–3pm. Breakfast only Friday to Sunday, dinner only Monday to Friday. Lunch daily. $
Beyond Words, in the 9th story of the Harold Washington Library. Monday 9am–6pm, Tuesday and Thursday 11am–6pm, Wednesday, Friday and Saturday 9am–4pm, closed Sunday. $

North of the Loop

Café Spiaggia and Spiaggia, 980 N. Michigan Avenue, tel: 312-280-2750. Daily 11.30am–10pm (Friday and Saturday until 11pm, Sunday until 9pm). Italian cuisine. $$$

Michael Jordan's The Restaurant, 500 N. LaSalle Street, tel: 312-644-3865. Sunday to Thursday 11.30am–10.30pm, Friday and Saturday 11.30am–midnight. A must for basketball fans. $$

Billy Goat Tavern, 430 N. Michigan Avenue (lower level), tel: 312-222-1525. For over 60 years the hunkiest cheeseburgers in town served here. Yellowing newspaper cuttings on the wall feature this famous haunt. $

Hard Rock Cafe, 63 W. Ontario Street, tel: 312-943-2252. Monday to Thursday 11.30am–midnight, Friday 11.30am–1am, Saturday 11am–1am, Sunday 11.30am–11pm. Rock'n'roll café with bar. In the city center. Signed photos, guitars, gold and platinum records by top groups displayed on the wall. Souvenir stores sells the inevitable T-shirts. Food served to loud musical accompaniment. $

Planet Hollywood, 663 N. Wells Street, tel: 312-266-7827. Sunday to Wednesday 10.30am–midnight, Thursday to Saturday 10.30am–1am. Another chain restaurant in Hollywood style with movie memorabilia. $

Ed's, 640 N. Wells Street, tel: 312-664-1707. Sunday to Thursday 11am–11pm, Friday and Saturday 11am–11.30pm. Fun bar with music and food. Themed afternoons or evenings (e.g. Tuesday is calypso afternoon). Snack meals served in noisy, hectic atmosphere. $

Big Shoulders Café, in the Museum of the Chicago Historical Society, 1601 N. Clark Street, tel: 312-587-7766. Coffee and cakes, salads and light pasta dishes. $

Café Brauer, 2021 Stockton Drive, tel: 312-280-2724/1217. In the summer, hours as Lincoln Park Zoo, in the winter Monday to Sunday 10am–3pm. $

Lakeview

Bella Vista, 1001 W. Belmont Avenue, tel: 773-404-0111. Monday to Saturday 11.30am–5pm (lunch), Monday to Thursday 5–10pm (dinner), Friday and Saturday 5–11pm, Sunday 5–10pm. A restaurant with several rooms in an old bank, imaginatively decorated with inlaid marble floors and frescoes on the walls. New Italian cuisine. Live jazz on Saturday from 6pm. $$

Intelligentsia, 3123 N. Broadway, tel: 773-348-8058. Monday to Thursday 6am–10pm, Friday 6am–11pm, Saturday 7am–11pm, Sunday 7am–10pm. Café with chairs outside. Roasts its own coffee beans. $

Lakefront Restaurant, 3042 N. Broadway, tel: 773-472-9040. Every day 6am–midnight. Over 30 years old; American cooking and sidewalk café under a pergola in Barry Street. Also vegetarian dishes. $

Billy Goat Tavern: the hunkiest cheeseburgers in town

Hard Rock Cafe

69

Restaurants all in a row

La Madeleine, 2813 N. Broadway, tel: 773-477-3173. Sunday to Thursday 7am–10pm, Friday and Saturday 7am–11pm. French dishes on a self-service basis. $

Hidden Shamrock, 2723 N. Halsted, tel: 773-883-0304. Every day 11am–2am. Noisy Irish bar, where all major sporting events, including soccer, are shown. Pool. Imported Irish, English and German beers. $

The beer that made Chicago famous

Scenes, 3168 N.Clark Street, tel: 773-525-1007. Sunday to Thursday 10.30am–11.30pm, Friday and Saturday 10.30am–2.30am. Small bookstore specializing in theater and movie literature. Tiny café. $

Ann Sather, 929 W. Belmont Avenue, tel: 773-348-2378. Sunday to Thursday 7am–10pm, Friday and Saturday 7am–11pm. Swedish restaurant chain, noted for its breakfasts (sweet rolls). $

Moti Mahal, 1035 W. Belmont Avenue, tel: 773-348-4392/3. Sunday to Thursday 11.30am–9.30pm, Friday and Saturday 11.30am–10.30pm. North Indian cuisine. $

Why not, 1059 W. Belmont Avenue, tel: 773-404-2800. Sunday to Thursday 9am–1am, Friday and Saturday 9am–2am. Café and second-hand bookstore in one. $

Buddies', 3301 N. Clark Street, tel: 773-477-4066. Monday to Thursday 7am–11pm, Friday and Saturday 9am–midnight, Sunday 9am–11pm. Good, international cuisine with gay waiters. Mostly for local gays and lesbians. $

El Jardín, 3401 N. Clark Street, tel: 773-935-8133. Sunday to Thursday 11am–10pm, Friday and Saturday 11am–2am. Mexican restaurant located deep in movie territory (*The Untouchables*) under the El. $

Hyde Park

The Medici, 1327 E. 57th Street, tel: 773-667-7394. Monday to Thursday 7am–11pm, Friday 7am–midnight, Saturday 9am–midnight, Sunday 9am–11pm. Also takeaway pizzas. $

Caffé Florian, 1450 E. 57th Street, tel: 773-752-4100. Sunday to Thursday 11am–midnight, Friday and Saturday 11am–1am. Busy, cramped restaurant with student clientele. Great pizzas, highly rated desserts. $

Hotel Florence Restaurant

Oak Park

Minou Café, 104 N. Marion Street, tel: 708-848-6540. Monday to Friday 7am–6pm, Saturday 8am–5pm, Sunday 8am–3pm. Home-made pastries and sandwiches. $

Java Joans, 119 N. Marion Street, tel: 708-524-JAVA or 4932. Monday to Thursday 7am–7pm, Friday and Saturday 7am–10pm. Wide variety of coffees and wines. $

Pullman

Hotel Florence Restaurant & Museum, 11111 S. Forrestville Avenue, tel: 773-785-8900. Monday to Friday

11am–2pm (lunch), Saturday 10am–2pm (continental breakfast), Sunday 10am–3pm (brunch). American home cooking. Old-fashioned setting. Booking essential for special Victorian gala dinners. $

The Retreat, 605 East 111th Street, tel: 773-568-6000. Tuesday to Friday 11am–2pm (lunch), Tuesday to Saturday 5–9pm (dinner), Saturday 11am–2pm (buffet), Sunday 11am–4pm (buffet). Closed Monday. Good selection of imported French wines. $$

Chinatown

Three Happiness, 2130 S. Wentworth, tel: 312-791-1228 and 209 W. Cermak, tel: 312-842-1964. Both Sunday to Thursday 9am–10pm, Friday and Saturday 9am–11pm. Specialty is dim sum. The restaurant in W. Cermak has a good atmosphere and local color, as you would expect in Chinatown. The newer restaurant is aimed at groups and is a little more expensive. $

The Saigon Vietnamese Restaurant & Shabu Shabu, 232 W. Cermak, tel: 312-808-1318. Daily 11am–3pm. *Shabu shabu*, a sort of fondue with fish, is this restaurant's specialty. Vietnamese, Chinese and Malaysian dishes. $

Dim sum is delightful

71

Pilsen

Nuevo León, 1515 W. 18th Street, tel: 312-421-1517. Monday to Thursday 8am–midnight, Friday and Saturday 8am–4am, Sunday 8am–1am. Good tamales. Specialty is sliced beef with tomatoes, peppers and onions. $

Los Comales No. 3, 1544 W. 18th Street, tel: 312-666-2251. Monday to Thursday 8am–midnight, Friday and Saturday 8am–4am, Sunday 8am–1am. Stylish fast food restaurant. Various types of breakfast eggs, plus burritos (large), tortas (medium) and tacos (small). $

Mexican remains a favorite

Late nite smoky sounds

Nightlife

Chicago is a city that never rests. In many areas, stores, bars and restaurants stay open for 24 hours and the range of cultural and sports events is huge. For details, see the listings magazine *Reader*. If you want quiet, evening entertainment, you are most likely to find it in the lobbies and lounges of the larger hotels, where you can sit in a comfortable armchair in elegant surroundings and enjoy the pianist or a jazz quartet. If you are looking for a little more excitement, seek out the bars in Rush Street or Division Street. Young sports fans will gravitate towards Wrigley Field or to Lakeview in the south, while those seeking gay activities will head for Belmont Avenue. Jazz and blues clubs can be located in fairly unsafe neighborhoods, so it's an idea to arrange for a cab there and back.

Jazz

Andy's, 11 E. Hubbard Street, tel: 312-642-6805. Evening sessions, but also top jazz bands on weekday lunch-times.
Cotton Club, 1710 S. Michigan Avenue, tel: 312-341-9787. Elegant club with predominantly black clientele. Pictures of jazz greats beam down from the wall.
The Green Mill, 4802 N. Broadway, tel: 773-878-5552. Formerly owned by Al Capone and frequented by his gang. Good jazz and on certain evenings the microphones are available for poets to recite their works.
Pops for Champagne, 2934 N. Sheffield Avenue, tel: 773-472-1000. Jazz with champagne. Mainly for yuppies.

Blues

Blues in the night

Blue Chicago, 736 N. Clark Street, tel: 312-642-6261, and **Blue Chicago on Clark**, 536 N. Clark Street, tel: 312-661-0100. A ticket will give you access to both blues clubs.

B.L.U.E.S., 2519 N. Halsted Street, tel: 773-528-1012, and **B.L.U.E.S. Etcetera**, 1124 W. Belmont Avenue, tel: 773-525-8989. Unpretentious blues clubs with performances every night.

Buddy Guy's Legends, 754 S. Wabash Avenue, tel: 312-427-0333. A club as you would imagine it from the movies. The band plays in the middle, surrounded by a long bar and pool tables and the whole thing in a smoky, dimly-lit room.

Checkerboard Lounge, 423 E. 43rd Street, tel: 773-624-3240. White students and black fans frequent this legendary club, where professional musicians play every night, long into the night.

Kingston Mines, 2548 N. Halsted Street, tel: 773-477-4646. Two bars with a youthful clientele.

Theater tickets

Tickets for theater, music and dance performances can be obtained on the day of the performance at half price, but you will have to go in person to one of the three offices of **Hot Tix** to collect and pay for them: 108 N. State Street, 700 N. Michigan Avenue and 2301 N. Clark Street. Monday to Saturday 10am–6pm, Sunday noon–5pm. Advance sales of full-price tickets for other performances are also available here. Other companies that sell tickets are **Ticketmaster**, tel: 312-559-121, **Fox Theatricals**, tel: 312-573-0050 or **Tower Tickets**, tel: 312-454-1300.

Theater

Goodman Theatre, 200 S. Columbus Drive, tel: 312-443-3800. Plays performed here often make it to Broadway.

Organic Theater, 3319 N. Clark Street, tel: 773-327-5588. Good theater which vacillates between improvisation, the experimental and the populist.

Steppenwolf Theater Company, 1650 N. Halsted Street, tel: 312-335-1650. One of the most successful theaters in the US. Founder and Hollywood star John Malkovich is sometimes in the cast.

Theater on the Lake, Fullerton & the lake, tel: 312-742-7994/5. Various theater groups perform here.

Classical music and musicals

Auditorium Theatre, 50 E. Congress Parkway, tel: 312-922-4046 or 312-922-2110. A successful musical often runs for months in this architectural gem, reckoned to have the best acoustics in Chicago.

Lyric Opera, 20 N. Wacker Drive, tel: 312-332-2244, fax: 312-332-0304. The leading opera house in Chicago with a predominantly classical repertoire.

Orchestra Hall, 220 S. Michigan Avenue, tel: 312-435-6666 or 312-294-3000. Where the famous Chicago Sym-

Steppenwolf Theater

Wonderful acoustics

phony Orchestra and its junior ensemble play regularly.
Merle Reskin Theater, 60 E. Balbo Avenue, tel: 312-922-1999. The Chicago Opera Theater Modern American composers often find an audience here.

Cabaret and comedy

Second City is first for comedy

Second City, 1616 N. Wells Street, tel: 312-337-3992. Second City helped put Chicago on the cultural map; for three decades the best comedians in town have entertained audiences here. John Belushi and Bill Murray polished their acts on this stage before heading out to Hollywood.

Cinemas

Biograph, 2433 N. Lincoln Avenue, tel: 773-348-4123. Historic cinema where Dillinger saw his last movie, before being gunned down by the FBI on the steps outside.
Music Box Theatre, 3733 N. Southport, tel: 773-871-6604. Beautiful old-fashioned movie house with premières, previews and classic American movies. Worth a visit for the interior décor alone.
The Vic, 3145 N. Sheffield, tel: 773-929-2739. Special evenings (usually Thursday) with cheap admission prices.

Clubs offering a range of entertainment

Excalibur, 632 N. Dearborn, tel: 312-266-1944. Sunday to Friday 5pm–4am, Saturday 5pm–5am. Pool, games room, restaurants, bars, cabaret, dancing etc. Thursday to Saturday live bands. Themed nights, e.g. Wednesday is alternative night, Thursday salsa. Admission fee for live music. Although the atmosphere is casual the dress code is semi-smart; men must wear shirts and pants.
Berlin, 954 W. Belmont Avenue, tel: 773-348-4975. Trendy dance club, mixed clientele, including gays and lesbians. Open every night until 4am.

Dillinger died here

74

Shopping

Downtown has its share of boutiques, fashion shops and galleries, along with several of America's best department stores. Chicago has enthusiastically embraced the concept of a shopping center and mall. A number of these can be recommended for the quality and variety of their shops, and for the exciting innovation of their design.

Two central shopping districts stand out above all others: **State Street** in the Loop, where Chicago's super-rich shop, and the **Magnificent Mile**, which draws shoppers and sightseers from all over the Midwest. Inside the Loop, the **Thompson Center** is noted for its fashion boutiques and **Wabash Avenue** for its jewelers. Along the Magnificent Mile, **Oak Street** is the place for designer fashions, but be prepared to pay for them.

The area for art galleries and antiques is to the north and east in **River North**. If you are in the market for second-hand clothes, antiques and bric-à-brac, the **Lincoln Park** district from Fullerton Avenue to Addison Street is the place to look. **Clark Street**, **Broadway** and **Belmont Avenue** have the highest concentration of stores. Book collectors will not be disappointed either.

The place for gold jewelry is a little further north. Many Asians have settled in **Devon Avenue** between Western Avenue and California Avenue, and they specialize not only in jewelry, but also textiles, handicrafts, spices, etc.

Lakeview and **Hyde Park** have plenty to offer bookworms, but booksellers and second-hand stores also abound in the area around the **University of Chicago**.

New Maxwell Street Market is flea market territory. Here you can expect to find upwards of 300 stalls selling everything from wheel trims to mouth-organs. Fruit and vegetable markets take place in the city center and at over 20 other sites in the suburbs from July to October. The so-called **Farmer's Markets** are held once a week, usually Saturday.

Fruits of the markets

Department stores

Marshall Field & Co., 111 N. State Street. Monday to Saturday 9.45am–7pm, Sunday noon–5pm. High-class shopping in sumptuous suroundings.
Carson Pirie Scott, 1 S. State Street. Monday to Friday 9.45am–7pm, Saturday 9.45am–6pm, Sunday noon–5pm. After Marshall Field, the biggest department store in the Loop. With eight floors, it is its equal in most respects.

Shopping centers and malls

Atrium Mall, 100 W. Randolph Street. Monday to Friday 8am–6pm, Saturday 11am–4pm. About 30 stores and restaurants open out on to a spectacular interior.

Water Tower Place

The Place for fine goods

Merchandise Mart, 300 N. Wells Street. Stores open and close at various times. Fifty boutiques and bars line the two lower floors of the Merchandise Mart, including fashions by Carson Pirie Scott and GAP.

Water Tower Place, 835 N. Michigan Avenue. Monday to Thursday 10am–7pm, Friday 10am–8pm, Saturday 10am–6pm, Sunday noon–6pm. Seven cinemas, over 150 stores and bars, including Marshall Field's second branch, Eddie Bauer and Laura Ashley.

Chicago Place, 700 N. Michigan Avenue. Monday to Friday 10am–7pm, Saturday 10am–6pm, Sunday noon–5pm. Over 50 stores, including Saks Fifth Avenue, keep all the latest fashions, cosmetics, etc.

900 North Michigan. Monday to Friday 10am–7pm, Saturday 10am–6pm, Sunday noon–6pm. New York chic at Bloomingdale's, Henri Bendel and about 60 other stores on six floors, plus two cinemas and six restaurants.

Century Shopping Center, 2828 N. Clark Street. In a converted theater with six floors; mainly clothing.

Gurnee Mills Outlet Mall, Interstate 94/Route 132 West (Grand Avenue), Gurnee. Monday to Saturday 10am–9pm, Sunday 11am–6pm. A vast center where over 200 discount stores compete with new special offers every day.

Antiques

The antique district is on the North Side in Lakeview and there are a number of stores and malls on W. Kinzie as well. Try **Belmont Antique Malls**, 2132 W. Belmont and 2227 W. Belmont; **Chicago Antique Centre**, 3045 N. Lincoln Avenue; **Jay Robert's Antique Warehouse** 149 W. Kinzie; **Lincoln Antique Mall**, 3141 N. Lincoln Avenue; **Wrigleyville Antique Mall**, 3336 N. Clark Street.

Bookstores

Barnes & Noble, many branches in Chicago, probably the best is at 659 W. Diversey Parkway. Every day 9am–11pm. Endless rows of shelves and a pleasant café.

Borders, several branches in Chicago, including one at 830 N. Michigan Avenue. Monday to Saturday 8am–11pm, Sunday 9am–9pm. Books and CDs. The café offers a fine view over the Magnificent Mile.

The Savvy Traveler, 310 S. Michigan Avenue. Monday to Saturday 10am–6pm. Great collection of travel guides.

Music

Jazz Record Mart, 444 N. Wabash Avenue. Monday to Saturday 10am–8pm, Sunday noon–5pm. Claims to have the biggest selection of jazz and blues in the world.

Chicago Music Mart, State Street/ Jackson Boulevard. Monday to Saturday 10am–6pm. A dozen or so stores selling everything for the music-lover.

A Sports-Mad Town

It was a Chicago sportsman who uttered the words 'it ain't over 'til the Fat Lady sings.' Chicago Bulls coach Dick Motta uttered this backhanded reference to opera to describe his team's hope in the face of despair, but since then the phrase has been used by everyone from movie stars to would-be gangsters to President Clinton on the eve of victory. Chicago sports fans are among the most enthusiastic in the world. They also have an enormous selection of sports from which to choose. Nowadays, before the Fat Lady sings, she can probably be found pondering whether to jog, cycle or rollerblade to the opera house.

Oak Street Beach

Swimming and beach activities

About 30 beaches by Lake Michigan have a lifeguard service operating from the end of May to the beginning of September (9am–9.30pm). The water in the lake warms up during the course of the summer and then the beaches are used for all sorts of other activities such as beach volleyball (now a near-Olympic sport) and frisbee.

Cycling and rollerblading

About 22 miles (35km) of lakeside paths have been widened for cyclists and rollerskaters and at weekends they come in droves. Cycles and rollerblades can be rented by the lake at **Bike Chicago**, tel: 1-800-915-BIKE (*see Tour 5, page 38*). The **Bike Shop** to the north, 1034 W. Belmont Avenue, tel: 773-868-6800 and **Wheels & Things** in the south, 5210 S.Harper Avenue, tel: 773-493-4326 only rent out bikes. **Londo Mondo Motionwear**, 1100 N. Dearborn Street, tel: 312-751-2794 and **City Sweats**, 2467 N. Clark Street, tel: 773-348-2489, specialize in rollerblades.

There are over 20 miles of lakeside paths to enjoy

Boating, canoeing, sailing and windsurfing

If you want to sit on a boat deck and see Chicago from the water, then excursions leave from beneath Michigan Avenue Bridge. From April to October, the **Wendella Sightseeing Boats** (tel: 312-337-1446) run trips along the Chicago River and out on the lake in the shadow of the downtown skyscrapers. The **Chicago Architecture Foundation** (tel: 312-922-3432 or 312-922-8687) organize guided tours through the streets and a very popular river trip with commentary. Advance booking is essential. Other boat trips leave from the Navy Pier.

If you want to take control on water, then canoes can be rented from **Chicagoland Canoe Base**, 4019 N. Narragansett Avenue, tel: 773-777-1489. Boats can be rented from the **Chicago Sailing Club** in Belmont Harbor, tel: 773-871-7245. Sailing courses are also offered. Windsurfers can rent boards from **Windward Sports**, 3317 N. Clark Street, tel: 773-472-6868, and courses are available. Montrose Harbor is another good spot for windsurfers and boards can be rented (tel: 773-878-3710).

Ship ahoy

Jogging and marathon

The many parks near the lake are great for jogging, but be careful at night and if jogging to the south of Soldier Field. Keep-fit apparatus is available in Lincoln Park up by Diversey Parkway. Marathon runners can take part in the October race. To register call 312-527-1105.

Jogging both indoors and out

Tennis and golf

You can play tennis at the Daley Bicentennial Plaza in Grant Park. Booking is essential. Tel: 312-742-7648. There are many golf courses in the Chicago area. Try the 9-hole **Illinois Center Golf Course** and Driving Range, 221 N. Columbus Drive, tel: 312-616-1234. Call 312-245-0909 to book time on any of the city's golf courses.

Pool and bowling

Many bars have a billiard table in a back room. Usually the game is pool and you play for money. **Chris's Billiards** has 40 tables at 4637 N. Milwaukee Street, tel: 773-286-4714. Pool is becoming a fad in discos, too, where pocketing the balls is rapidly taking over from sweating it out on the dance floor. There are numerous bowling alleys in the city, too. At **Southport Lanes & Billiards**, you still have to pick up the pins by hand. The biggest bowling alley (possibly in the world) is the **Miami Bowl**, 5023 Archer Street, tel: 773-585-8787, which has 80 lanes and stays open around the clock. Many people use the bowl as much as a social center as a sports center, arranging to meet early in the evening, stopping for a bite to eat, and only leaving late into the night.

Spectator sports

Tickets for all spectator sports are available at the stadiums themselves or from **Ticketmaster**, tel: 312-559-1212.

Cubs crazy

Baseball
The baseball season lasts from April to October. The White Sox (American League) play in the park that bears their name. The Cubs (National League) play at Wrigley Field, one of the oldest and most-loved stadiums in the US. Built in 1916, there was a local outcry in 1989 when the men who run the field bowed to modern economics and installed lights which allowed night games to be played.

Football
The Bears play at Soldier Field, the stadium where soccer's World Cup matches were played. The season lasts from September to December.

Basketball and ice hockey
The Chicago Bulls are the city's pride and joy. Spearheaded by Michael Jordan, the Bulls have gone from strength to strength. Every time the team wins a major title, Chicagoans seem to rediscover their southern European roots and drive through the city, horns blaring. The Bulls play in the United Center, which they share with the Black Hawks ice hockey team.

The Bulls can't be beat

79

Soccer
Soccer is fast gaining in popularity. The city now has its own team, the Chicago Stingers. Their symbol is a wasp and they play at The Hive in Forest View Park, 2121 S. Goebbert Road in Arlington Heights. For information about tickets, call 847-670-5425.

Football fans are rarely disappointed

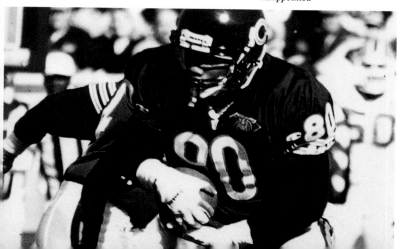

Getting There and Around

Opposite: have music, will travel

By air

International flights usually arrive at O'Hare International Airport (tel: 773-686-2200), which is about 16 miles (25 km) from the city center. Chicago Midway Airport (tel: 773-767-0500) is used by most domestic services. The cheapest way into Chicago from either airport is on CTA-operated trains. Blue line trains from O'Hare leave every 15 minutes around the clock (half-hourly or hourly at night; journey time: 45 minutes). Orange line trains leave from Midway every 10 minutes, Monday to Saturday, 5am–11.30pm. On Sunday and holidays, the service starts at 7.30am (journey time: 30 minutes).

A taxi journey into the city center takes between 40 minutes or an hour depending on the traffic. A taxi share scheme is in operation both here and at Midway, from where the journey into the center takes about half an hour. The Airport Express bus links O'Hare Airport with the city center (daily 5am–11.30pm) and with the north of the city (daily 5am–8.30pm). The Midway airport bus service runs daily 5.15am–10.30pm. All the major car rental firms have desks at the airport.

Airport express

81

Public transportation

The Chicago Transit Authority (CTA) operates a network of bus, elevated and underground rail services. Stations, hotels and tourist information offices keep maps showing the scheduled public transportation services. Some trains and bus routes run for 24 hours. Tokens for buses and trains are sold in packs of 10 at banks, bureaux de change and some supermarkets. Machines inside the buses 'swallow' the token or a $1 dollar note and the corresponding number of coins. If you change trains and continue in the same direction within the network, no supplement is required, but if you want to change buses or change from train to bus (or vice versa), at the start of your journey you have to pay an extra fee for a transfer ticket. Visitors can purchase tickets valid for the whole CTA network. Available are 1, 2, 3 or 5 day passes, obtainable at the airports, the Union Station, tourist information offices, attractions and selected hotels.

Elevated transportation

Taxis

Taxis can be hailed from the sidewalk or, in the quieter parts of the city, can be ordered by phone (Yellow Cabs, tel: 312-829-4222 or Checker Taxi, tel: 312-243-2537). The meter in all cabs is set so that the first mile costs $1.50 and each subsequent mile $1.20. Every extra passenger adds 50¢ per mile and the driver will expect a tip of between 10 and 15 percent of the full fare

Taxis take you anywhere

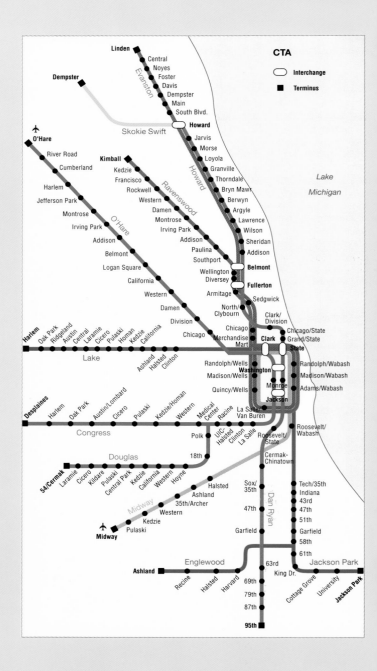

Facts for the Visitor

Tourist Information

The city's main tourist office is the **Chicago Office of Tourism**, Chicago Cultural Center, 78 E. Washington Street, Chicago, Il 60602, tel: 312-744-2400, for the hard of hearing, tel: 312-744-2947. To obtain a brochure, call 1-800-2CONNECT and to make a hotel reservation, call the Illinois Reservation Service on 1-800-978-7890 or 312-640-0637.

Other branches of the tourist board are as follows: **Chicago's Historic Water Tower Visitor Welcome Center**, Chicago and Michigan Avenue, tel: 312-440-3165. Monday to Friday 9.30am–6pm, Saturday 10am–6pm, Sunday 11am–5pm. In summer, all closing times are one hour later; **Chicago Cultural Center Visitor Information Center**, 77 E. Randolph Street, tel: 312-346-3278. Monday to Friday 10am–6pm, Saturday 10am–5pm, Sunday noon–5pm; **Illinois Market Place Visitor Information Center**, 700 E. Grand Avenue (in the Navy Pier), tel: 312-832-0010. Monday to Thursday 10am–9pm, Friday and Saturday 10am–10pm, Sunday 10am–7pm.

Info from the Water Tower

Opening times

Stores are usually open Monday to Saturday 10am–6pm. Bank hours are Monday to Friday 9am–3pm, but post offices open Monday to Friday 8am–6pm, Saturday 8am–noon. Many stores stay open in the evening, on Sunday and some never close. Most museums are closed all day on Tuesday.

Time

Central Standard Time (CST) applies in Chicago. When it is noon Standard Time in Chicago, it is 6pm in London. 'Daylight Saving Time', i.e., when clocks are advanced by one hour, applies from the beginning of April to the end of October.

Public holidays

New Year's Day (Jan 1); Martin Luther King Day (3rd Monday in January); Presidents' Day (3rd Monday in February); Memorial Day (last Monday in May); Independence Day (July 4); Labor Day (1st Monday in September); Columbus Day (2nd Monday in October); Veterans' Day (November 11); Thanksgiving (4th Thursday in November); Christmas Day (December 25).

If a fixed holiday falls on a Sunday, the following Monday usually counts as the holiday. Most state and government offices, museums and post offices are closed on national holidays. Stores and shopping malls stay open and many have sales at these times.

Travel documents

International travelers should bring a valid passport. No visa is required if your length of stay does not exceed 90 days and you can furnish a valid return ticket. If you want to stay longer, apply for a visa at the US Consulate.

Length of stay is determined by the immigration officer you meet on arrival, so it's a good idea to have ready such things as credit cards, traveler's checks or hotel reservation forms if requested to do so.

Tipping

In restaurants, service tends not to be included within the price, but it is usual to leave a sum equivalent to about 15 percent of the bill on the table or to add it to the credit card slip. This sum should not be regarded as a tip but as payment for the service provided. A hotel porter gets about $1–2 for each item of luggage, taxi-drivers and hairdressers expect 10 to 15 percent of the bill and it is customary to leave the hotel chambermaid $1–2 for each day stayed.

Service with a smile

Voltage

110 volts AC. An adapter will be necessary for European electrical appliances such as shavers and hairdryers.

Telephones

Making local calls is easy: lift the receiver, insert 25¢ and dial the seven-digit number. To find out the numbers of people or places, dial 411. To make long-distance calls, dial 0 for the operator. Direct dialing is possible, if the full area code is known. Overseas calls can also be made by direct dialing, but if you're calling from a pay phone your pockets will have to be stuffed full of quarters. The code for the UK is 011 44, followed by the area code minus

Phone home from here

the initial zero; Australia's code is 011 61 and New Zealand's 011 64; for Canada just dial the area code and the number. The area code for central Chicago is 312.

Alcohol

As a rule, alcoholic drinks (and that includes beer) are only sold to anyone age 21 or over and identity card checks in clubs and bars are usually made. Beer and wine may be bought in food stores, but stronger drinks are available only in liquor stores.

It is an offense to drink alcohol in a car. Open bottles must be kept in the trunk.

Medical assistance

To find the addresses of doctors, dentists and hospitals, consult the Yellow Pages telephone directory. Medicine is available in the pharmacies on the main shopping streets or at drugstores in large supermarkets. Some 17 branches of Walgreen's are open 24 hours, including the one at 757 N. Michigan Avenue, tel: 312-664-8686. Call Osco Drugs on 1-800-654-6726 at any time of day (toll-free) and you can find out where the nearest branch is.

The best hospital with a 24-hour accident and emergency service is the Northwest Memorial Hospital, 233 E. Superior, tel: 312-908-200. To summon an ambulance, call 911. For a private ambulance, call the Vandenberg Ambulance Service.

Only in emergencies

Emergencies

Within Chicago, call 911 for the police, fire department, highway patrol or emergency doctor. Otherwise, contact a telephone operator for emergency help by dialing 0.

Disabled

Disabled visitors can obtain information before they leave home by writing to The Mayor's Office for People with Disabilities, Room 405B, 510 N. Peshtigo Court, Chicago, Il 60611. Call 312-744-6673, Monday to Friday 8.30am–4.30pm. Information also available on 312-744-4016.

Crime

Chicago is as safe or as unsafe as any other American city and it is important to be vigilant. Be on guard in Pilsen, in Hyde Park and in the Loop at night, but Michigan Avenue and the northern neighborhoods are regarded as safer. Generally speaking, you will be most at risk in the southern and western districts of the city.

The boys in blue

When traveling through the more remote parts of the city, lock your car internally. If you get lost in what looks like one of the run-down areas, try to get back on to a main road as quickly as possible.

Where to Stay

Overnight accommodation in Chicago is not cheap. Apart from the room price and tax, tips for staff have to be included. As in restaurants, the room maid ($2 per day), the porter ($2 per item of baggage) and the bellman ($1 per call) rely on these gratuities to supplement their wages. For business travelers and wealthy tourists, Chicago can offer many grand hotels, most of which are on the Magnificent Mile. Visitors with less generous budgets will also find an increasing number of possibilities as Chicago hoteliers gradually adjust to the pockets of students and less well-heeled overseas guests. At weekends and outside peak seasons, many hotels offer special deals.

Room reservations

Hot Rooms, tel: 773-468-7666 or 1-800- 468-3500, fax: 312-649-0559 (includes the Blackstone Hotel, Lenox Suites, The Westin); **Chicago Hotel Room Reservations,** tel: 214-361-7311 or 1-800-964-6835, fax: 214-361-7299; **Bed & Breakfast Chicago Inc.,** tel: 312-951-0085, fax: 312-649-9243.

Hotel selection

The following suggestions are listed according to three categories: $$$ = expensive (from $200); $$ = moderate ($100–200); $ = inexpensive (up to $100).

In and by the Loop

The Swissôtel

Swissôtel, 323 E. Wacker Drive, tel: 312-565-0565 or 1-800-654-7263, fax: 312-565-0540. Luxury hotel in a glass-walled skyscraper. Good views of the lakeside and city center. Swimming pool; fitness room with view. $$$

The Blackstone Hotel, 636 S. Michigan Avenue, tel: 312-427-4300 or 1-800-622-6330, fax: 312-427-4736. Hotel with a view over Grant Park. Old-fashioned interior often used as a backdrop for movies. $$

Palmer House Hilton. 17 E. Monroe Street, tel: 312-726-7500 or 1-800-445-8667, fax: 312-263-2556 or 312-917-1707. Hotel with 1639 rooms, 88 suites, five restaurants, bar, indoor pool and fitness room. A slightly nostalgic feel. Impressive lobby (*see page 20*). $$

Putting on the Ritz

Hotels north of the Loop

The Ritz-Carlton, 160 E. Pearson Street, tel: 312-266-1000 or 1-800-621-6906, fax: 312-266-1194. A luxury hotel with a tropical-style lobby on the 12th floor of Water Tower Place. Swimming pool, piano music in the winter garden, excellent restaurant (*see page 37*). $$$

Hotel Inter-Continental, 505 N. Michigan Avenue, tel: 312-944-4100 or 1-800-628-2112, fax: 312-944-3050. Luxury hotel with old-fashioned charm. Fin-de-siècle indoor pool. $$$

Drake Hotel, 140 E. Walton Place, tel: 312-787-2200 or 1-800-527-4727, fax: 312-951-5803. A lavish lobby worth visiting even if you're not staying in this landmark 1920s hotel *(see page 38)*. $$

Gold Coast Guest House, 113 W. Elm Street, tel: 312-337-0361, fax: 312-337-0362. Nice, clean pension with only five rooms. By the Magnificent Mile. Friendly service and attractive garden. $$

Surf, 555 W. Surf, tel: 773-528-8400 or 1-800-SURF-108, fax: 773-528-8483. Relatively peaceful spot in the Lakeview neighborhood. Rooms with a hint of Paris. $

Cass Hotel, 640 N. Wabash Avenue, tel: 312-787-4030 or 1-800-CASS-850, fax: 312-787-8544. In the hotel quarter. Good value. $

Exterior detail from the Hotel Inter-Continental

The Drake Hotel

In Oak Park
Wright's Cheney House B & B, 520 N. East Avenue, Oak Park, tel: 708-524-2067, fax: 312-236-0860. $

The Carleton of Oak Park, 1110 Pleasant Street, tel: 708-848-5000, fax: 708-848-0537. $

Hostels
Arlington House, 616 W. Arlington Place, tel: 1-800-HOSTEL-5 or 773- 929-5380, fax: 773-665-5485. Youth hostel in a good location for the city center and the northern entertainment area. Open 24 hours a day. Use of kitchen. Mixed and segregated bedrooms. $

Chicago International Hostel, 6318 N. Winthrop Avenue, tel: 773-262-1011. In the north and rather off the beaten track. Good connections to the city center via the Loop. Use of kitchen, family rooms. $

HI-Chicago Summer Hostel, 731 S. Plymouth Court, tel: 773-327-5350, fax: 773-327-4287. Open 7am–midnight. For further information, ring the above number. Special program for guests includes reduced price sailing trips, free blues evenings, etc. $

HI-International House of Chicago, 1414 E. 59th Street, tel: 773-753-2270, fax: 773-753-1227. Hostel on the University of Chicago campus. $

Index

Adler Planetarium 45
Art Deco 29
Art Institute of
    Chicago...................33
Arthur B. Heurtley
    House.....................54
Auditorium Building ...32

Baseball.....................79
basketball 79
Belmont Harbor 41–2
Berghoff, The 21
Bicycle Museum
    of America...............44
Billy Goat Tavern ...35–6
Bootleg Homes............54
Buckingham Fountain.44

Cabrini Green...............8
cafés 67
Capone, Al 11, 13
Carbide and Carbon
    Building..................18
Carson Pirie Scott and
    Company store....20, 61
Charles E. Roberts
    House.....................53
Chess Pavilion.............40
Chicago Board of
    Trade Building..........29
Chicago Cultural
    Center..................34–5
Chicago Historical
    Society...................40
Chicago Lyric Opera...26
Chicago Place...............37
Chicago River`
    ....6, 12, 17, 24–5
Chicago School
    ....19, 20, 21, 29
Chicago Theater..........19
Chicago Tribune
    Tower....................35
Chinatown................58–9
Civic Opera House 26
climate.........................7
Columbian
    Exposition.....12, 19, 35
Court Theater 50
Cummings Life Science
    Center....................50
cycling.......................78

Daley, Richard J....10, 13
Daley Center 23
Daley Plaza 22–3
Dillinger, John............13
Diversey Harbor.........41

Economy.......................9
Edwin H. Cheney
    House.....................53
Enrico Fermi Institute .50
Ernest Hemingway
    Museum..................52
Ernest Hemingway's
    Birthplace 53

Farm in the Zoo..........40
Federal Center 21
Federal Plaza 21–2
festivals and shows .64–5
Field Museum of
    Natural History.....44–5
Fine Arts Building.......30
First National Bank 22
Fisher Building............30
football 79
Fort Dearborn 17
Frank Lloyd Wright
    Home and Studio......54

George W. Furbeck
    House..................52–3
Grant Park 44
Great Fire 12, 61
Greenstone Church......57

Harold Washington
    Library Center 32
Haymarket Riot...........12
Henry S. Adams House53
history 12–13

Ida Noyes Hall 48
International House .47–8
International Style........61

Jahn, Helmut...22, 26, 62
James R. Thompson
    Center 23
Jardine Water
    Purification Plant......43
Jazz and Blues...63, 72–3
Jenney, William
    Le Baron 30–1, 61
John Hancock
    Center 38, 62
Jordan, Michael...........13

Laboratory Schools 48
LaSalle Street 27
Leiter Building II 32
Lincoln Park Zoo 41
London Guarantee
    Building..................18
Loop, The 17–33

Madison Plaza
    Complex 26–7
Magnificent Mile 34–8
Manhattan Building 30
Marina City 25
Marquette
    Jacques 12, 17
Marquette Building 21
Marshall Field and
    Company store.........19
McCormick Place........46
Merchandise Mart 25
Metropolitan
    Correctional Center ..31
Michael Jordan's
    Restaurant.......25, 69
Michigan Avenue
    Bridge 17–18
Monadnock Building ...30
Montrose Harbor.........42
movies 63
Museum of
    Contemporary Art 37
Museum of Science
    and Industry............46
music venues...........73–4

Nathan Moore House...54
Nature Museum...........44
Navy Pier 43
neighborhoods..............8
nightlife..................72–4
North Pier...................44
North Pond 41

Oak Park 51–4
Oak Street Beach.........40
Old Colony Building...30
One West Wacker
    Drive......................26
Orchestra Hall 33
Oriental Institute 49

Palmer House..............20
Peggy Notebaert
    Nature Museum of the
    Chicago Academy of
    Sciences..................41
Pilsen.........................59
Playboy Building 38
politics...................9–10
poverty 8
Prairie House Style .51–4
Printer's Row 31
Prohibition.................11
Pui Tak Center 59
Pullman 55–6
Pullman, George ...12, 56

Reliance
    Building..............19–20
restaurants 68–71
Robie House................49
Rockefeller Memorial
    Chapel....................48
Rookery Building....27–8
R. R. Donnelley
    Center.................24–5
Rush Street 38

Sears Tower 13, 28, 62
Shedd Aquarium 45
shopping 75–6
Sinclair, Upton ...5, 9, 12
skyscrapers 62
Smart Museum.............50
Soldier Field...............46
Solidarity Drive...........46
St Valentine's Day
    Massacre.............11, 13
State Street 19–20
stockyards 9,
Stone Container
    Building..................35
Sullivan,
    Louis H.......20 , 32, 61

Taylor Homes..............58
Terra Museum of
    American Art............36
Theater on the Lake.....42
theaters 73
tourist information 83

Unity Temple...............52
University of
    Chicago..............47–50
University Quadrangle 49

Van der Rohe,
    Ludwig Mies 21, 61

Wacker Drive 26
Water Tower 37
Water Tower
    Place................37–8, 62
watersports 78
White Sox Stadium 58
William E. Martin
    House.....................53
Wright, Frank
    Lloyd 12, 27, 51–4
Wrigley Building 35

Xerox Building 22

Zoo.......................40–1